DARK
HISTORY
of RUSSIA

DARK HISTORY of RUSSIA

Crime, Corruption and Murder in the Motherland

MICHAEL KERRIGAN

amber
BOOKS

Published by Amber Books Ltd
United House
London N7 9DP
United Kingdom
www.amberbooks.co.uk
Instagram: amberbooksltd
Facebook: www.facebook.com/amberbooks
Twitter: @amberbooks

ISBN: 978-1-78274-631-7

Project Editor: Sarah Uttridge
Designer: Jeremy Williams
Picture Researcher: Terry Forshaw

Printed in China

Contents

NOTES FROM UNDERGROUND

Violence, death and darkness have been built into the very foundations of the Russian state, the only real constant of two millennia of history.

GAGGING, gasping for breath through the scrunched-up fabric stuffing his frantic mouth, the little boy could no more speak than he could move. Tightly trussed with cord, a sobbing, shuddering, quivering bundle, he lay in the same foetal tuck that he had assumed in his mother's womb a few short years before.

The village community, gathered around, looked on with awed respect, but no sympathy. The boy's mother had been a foreigner – a slave – and the gods' work was being done. As the priest pulled harder on the garrotting leash and the victim's life struggle subsided, the prevailing mood was of an obligation met, of an auspicious start. With a gravelly slither and a muffled thud, the inert body fell into the deep pit before them. The men stood braced: now they could get to work raising the roof-post around which the new house would be built.

Later, anthropologists might choose to see their work as symbolic, this human sacrifice a spiritual acknowledgement of

Opposite: Lenin's Communists were 'red' in acknowledgement of the sacrifices made by previous revolutionaries – but the whole of Russian history has been soaked in blood.

Above: Fyodor Dostoyevsky's was a gloomy muse but a deeply illuminating one. No writer has shown more insight into the darker corners of the Russian consciousness.

the roof-post's central role as an *axis mundi* – an 'axis of the world'. Connecting the three realms – this earth, the underworld, and the heavens above – it would represent the overall harmony of the universe in which they dwelt. Less reflective, perhaps, and certainly less articulate in the language of 21st-century scholarship, the early Slavs knew that what they had done was fitting. The gods required this offering in return for their favour. If the gods were to watch over this house, they were entitled to a sacrifice.

UP FROM BELOW

'Every man has reminiscences which he would not tell to everyone, but only to his friends,' remarks the narrator in Fyodor Dostoyevsky's novella *Notes from Underground* (1864). 'He has other matters in his mind which he would not reveal even to his friends, but only to himself, and that in secret. But there are other things which a man is afraid to tell even to himself...'

What goes for men appears to go for nations too. The collective reminiscence, that is history, tends to be a more or less upbeat narrative – but darker episodes refuse to be suppressed. The Russian story stands apart, however, in being shot through with tragedy and violence at nearly every stage of its existence. This, it seems, is a country whose whole history has been 'dark'. By no means short of achievements, dramatic victories and great personalities, it has been by turns bleak and blood-sodden, tragic and grotesque.

At its best, the history of Russia has been characterized by cruelty and ruthlessness. Ivan the Terrible took the tyrannical violence of an absolute monarchy to its most monstrous lengths. Although in their different ways both worthy of the honorific, the two 'great' Czars, Peter I and Catherine II, were living caricatures, embodying the excesses of untrammelled authority.

Whether under czars or communist officials, Russia was to prosper in oppression. In its imperial splendour, it was carried by the cruelly exploited serfs. The depth of their servitude was arguably equalled, the sadism of their treatment almost certainly surpassed by the punishments dealt out to those deemed hostile to the dictatorship of Stalin from the 1920s on. With the most generous possible assessment, the achievements of communism were secured at an appalling human cost: some would insist that the Soviet experiment was anti-human by its nature.

HUMAN SACRIFICE

Russia's greatest historic triumphs have been attained in the sort of adversity that calls into question the victory that was secured. It was a self-destructive heroism that saw off French invaders in 1812 and Hitler's German army in what Russians came to call the 'Great Patriotic War'.

The country was self-destructive not just literally – in the burning of Moscow and the starvation endured by the citizens of Leningrad – but spiritually as well. Some sort of scorched earth of the soul enabled the Russian people to prevail by soaking up more suffering than their attackers could ultimately inflict; their subsequent celebrations were also times of deepest mourning.

Why should this be? Does Russian history labour under some kind of curse? Many Russians have felt this way down the generations. Rational analysis would hardly be expected to uphold such a conclusion. At the same time, though, where there has been so long and harrowing a history of suffering, the idea has acquired a certain mythic force.

HEALTH WARNING

If Russia's history has been written in blood, it has also been written in a spirit of profound partisanship. For much of modernity, the country has been seen as menacing the West. It is generally accepted now, for example, that successive US administrations of the Cold War era talked

Below: Ivan the Terrible holds up the Orthodox Christian cross under which he (at least nominally) fought.

up the Soviet nuclear threat. (They didn't *make* it up, but they massively exaggerated Russia's military power and reach.) Western politicians and media were never slow to criticize Russian policy, at home or in the wider world, or to attack the USSR's disdain for human rights. Left-wing commentators pointed out that those same politicians and media were not half so perturbed when comparable attitudes were shown and equivalent crimes committed by US clients.

They were right: as 'free' as the Western media might have been, a certain collectivity of interests and assumptions assisted in what the linguist and peace campaigner Noam Chomsky called the 'manufacture of consent'. Without the White House, Downing Street, the Élysée Palace or anyone else cracking the censor's whip, the Western media more or less fell into line with the view coming out of these centres of Western power.

Below: A clean-cut commissar wags a warning finger at a top-hatted, plutocratic-looking United States: he should reconsider his race to nuclear arms, or face the consequences... (1948).

COLD WAR RENEWED?

To some degree, the same stance has been true in the post-Communist period, certainly since the onset of what some call 'Cold War II'. It has been said that the collapse of the Western banking system in 2008 emboldened Vladimir Putin's Russia, encouraging it to rise above its own economic difficulties and start throwing its global weight around again. It can hardly be disputed that Russia has re-emerged as a mover and shaker on the world stage – although, in fairness, this was to have been expected once the turbulence following the collapse of communism had been weathered.

Up to a point, moreover, this is also justifiable: Russia has its own regional interests around the Black Sea, in the Caucasus and the Middle East. Why wouldn't it want to defend them? As in Cold War I, the question comes down to how far we think Russia seeks to go beyond its own legitimate, immediate security interests to interfere in the affairs of the wider world. As in Cold War I, we have seen signs of journalistic attitudes towards Russia increasingly divided between hawkish hostility and 'dove'-ish sympathy. It can be hard to know which view is right. To make matters more complicated, these divisions have not necessarily occurred along the left–right ideological lines that prevailed before.

Above: Russia was as badly hit as anywhere by the financial crisis of 2008–9, though it was able to exploit ensuing global problems to its own ends.

DEMOCRATIC DEFICIT

If Western commentary on Russia should often be taken with a grain of salt, Russia's rulers have historically lied freely. Nor have they had any truck with those ideas of official accountability and press freedom that Western governments have espoused (theoretically, at least). Under Communism, indeed, information management was weaponized. In the face of the world's hostility, officials felt justified in deploying propaganda in the pretence that it was news.

But then, the USSR barely made the most minimal pretence of democratic freedom. The workers around whose efforts and requirements the whole society had supposedly been organized did not have the right to unionize, own their homes or travel freely, and were generally much less materially well-off than their 'oppressed' and 'exploited' brothers and sisters in capitalist countries. Political dissent was not tolerated; nor was any expression of opinion outside the institutions of the state.

Critics of the Soviet order could be harassed – or, of course, sent off to labour camps.

Despite the use of worthy-sounding terminology (the word *soviet* itself denoted an elected workplace council; the Supreme Soviet or Congress was ostensibly their collective voice), the absence of any real opposition meant that the Communist Party's ruling committee, the Politburo, exercised a degree of control over the country that the Czars could only have envied. A former lieutenant colonel of the Soviet Secret Police, the KGB, Vladimir Putin, Russia's premier throughout the present century, has not shown himself to be especially invested in either press freedom or political plurality.

ABSOLUTE POWER

If we look for continuities between the Communist and the Czarist eras, we can most convincingly find it in the tendency of those with power to wield it absolutely. If there has been a curse upon Russian history, it has been that seemingly deep-seated instinct in those in charge that opposition was not to be tolerated. The notorious gulags of the Communist era carried on the work of the *katorga* camps to which criminals and dissidents had been sent since the 17th century. This was in its turn the consequence of structural problems in the polity as a whole. Historically, Russia had been held back by the weakness of any but the highest, most overarching, offices of state and the lack of an intermediate tier between the central authority and the masses.

Over the centuries, Western European societies had been building complexity, accumulating 'squirearchies' – influential lobbies of substantial farmers, rural professions, entrepreneurs and middle-class elites in the smaller towns and larger cities. Their demands, and their defence of their interests, acted to some extent as an inhibition on the freedom of action of the great landowners and the monarchies above them. These systems were anything but egalitarian, but they dished out their unfairness more equitably than the Russian Czarist system did.

THESE SYSTEMS WERE ANYTHING BUT EGALITARIAN, BUT THEY DISHED OUT THEIR UNFAIRNESS MORE EQUITABLY THAN THE RUSSIAN CZARIST SYSTEM.

Opposite: 'Death to the World Imperialist Monster': Soviet workers fight the forces of capitalist exploitation in this spectacular poster by Dmitry Moor (1883–1946).

Above: Camp inmates labour to construct the North Pechora Railway in the Komi region of Arctic Siberia: thousands were to die in unspeakable conditions on such schemes.

FROM THE HOUSE OF THE DEAD

'Where are the primary causes on which I am to build?' asked Dostoyevsky's narrator in *Notes from Underground*. 'Where are my foundations? Where am I to get them from?' In pagan times, Slavic custom demanded that a human sacrifice be offered at the start of any major construction; that a slave – often a child – be immured within the wall or floor of a new house. Towards the end of the first millennium, the Orthodox Church explicitly forbade this practice in its *Nomocanon* (Canon Law): 'May he who places a human being be punished with twelve years of penitence and three hundred genuflections. Let a wild boar, bull or goat be placed instead.'

But the memory was to endure – as, apparently, was the practice; the folklorist Mikhail I. Popov (1742–90) recorded it well into the 18th century. Dostoyevsky surely recalled this in his creation of a strange and sinister speaking voice from beneath the floorboards – a voice that, in its self-degrading eloquence, seems to speak for Russia too. The house of Russian history was, it seems, all but literally founded on human sacrifice; the bodies of the dead are built into its very fabric.

This book will not attempt to argue that Russia is an accursed country, nor that its people have been collectively condemned to suffering by some centuries-old pathology. But the most dispassionate perspective on Russia's past can hardly ignore the violence and turbulence, the chronic cruelty and suffering that seem to have dogged its history more or less throughout.

THE SUNGHIR SACRIFICE

SOME OF THE FIRST Russians we know of seem to have been ritually slaughtered. The bodies of a boy and girl unearthed by archaeologists at Sunghir, some 193km (120 miles) east of Moscow, brought with them their own notes from underground.

The two children, seemingly sacrificed some 30,000 years ago in the Upper Paleolithic period, had been placed head to head beside two adult corpses. Both victims had been physically disabled: the boy a dwarf, the girl's skeleton showing shortened and bent thighbones. Their differences seem to have marked them out for sacrifice.

We should not conclude that they were social rejects, however. Archaeologists point out that their 'abnormal' features may have given them an exalted status. The more important the person, the more significant was the sacrifice. This would tally with the treatment of their bones with red ochre, made of clay, and the sewing of some 5000 ivory beads into their leather caps and clothes. They also had ornaments of Arctic fox teeth and pendants of semi-precious stones, along with exquisitely carved ivory pins: they certainly had not been casually thrown away.

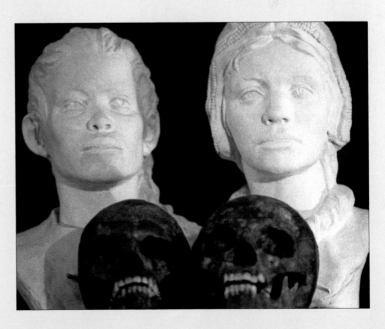

Right: Anthropological reconstruction has allowed us to see the Sunghir Children's faces.

1

'THE EXPANSES ARE SO GREAT...': KIEVAN RUS

Russia has always seemed very dark and disorientating in proportion to its vastness – as much to its own people, it seems, as to outsiders.

'GREAT HATRED, little room, maimed us at the start.' This straightforward explanation of his native Ireland's wretched history offered by the poet W.B. Yeats (1865–1939) could serve for many other countries. Time and again, a sense of claustrophobia seems to have intensified ethnic and religious rivalries in societies around the world. Russia, however, has never had that problem.

AN AGORAPHOBIC AGONY
Russia has long been, by some distance, the world's biggest country geographically, and that literal sense of spatial confinement would never have been felt. A character in Nikolai Gogol's (1809–52) famous play *The Government Inspector* (1836) says of the small provincial town in which the scene

Opposite: Rurik and his successor Oleg were effectively the founders of the Russian state. They are commemorated by this memorial in Staraya Ladoga, north of Volkhov.

is set: 'Even if you ride for three years you won't come to any other country.'

This is an impressive claim, but unsettling in its implications. How can a country so big and so comparatively empty provide anything in the way of a real 'home'? How could anyone find a psychological anchorage in this all but endless space?

Anton Chekhov (1860–1904), another Russian writer – and a practicing doctor too – diagnosed the vastness of his country as an important influence on its people's mental health. 'In Western Europe people perish from the congestion and stifling closeness,' he wrote in a letter to a friend (5 February 1888), 'but with us it is from the spaciousness. The expanses are so great that the little

Below: A group of hikers make their way across a slope in Central Asia's Saylyugem Mountains. The Russian landscape is mesmerizing in its sheer vastness.

man hasn't the resources to orientate himself...This is what I think about Russian suicides.'

At more than three times the global average, Russia's suicide rate continues to shock, but psychologists haven't generally agreed with Chekhov's theory. At a more poetic level, however, it has the ring of truth. A sense of disorientation might always have been intrinsic to the Russian consciousness. The only country coalesced slowly out of what had been more or less empty and frontierless space. Where Western Europe's countries are often clearly demarcated by natural features – rivers, mountain ranges or switches in landscape type – no such natural frontiers fence in the vastness of the Eurasian Steppe. Often described as a 'sea of grass', this semi-arid plain extends over 8000km (5000 miles) between Manchuria's Pacific coast and the Hungarian plain (*Puszta*) in the west.

> HOW CAN A COUNTRY SO BIG AND SO COMPARATIVELY EMPTY PROVIDE ANYTHING IN THE WAY OF A REAL 'HOME?

PASTORAL VALUES

It was not only Russia's physical but its human geography that seemed so open, indefinite, fluid and amorphous. As if to underline the absence of natural boundaries – or of anything much to interrupt the endless sweep of waving grass and sparser semi-desert – its population was for centuries mostly nomadic. As herding communities, they had to be.

In Western tradition, pastoral life has, since classical times, been seen as quintessentially quiet and peaceful. The original 'idylls' – poems by Theocritus (*c.*270 BCE) – described the innocent and essentially carefree lives and loves of shepherds. The reality of life for the nomadic pastoralists of the steppes was very different. That ocean of grass once viewed up close looked much less lush: pastoralism was, by its very nature, nomadic. Communities had to be ready to move at a moment's notice to get the best out of locally variable grazing and water supplies, and this meant the need for enormous areas of territory to be protected.

Above: The 'Farmers of the Steppe' in this old engraving now seem quintessentially Russian: for centuries, though, these endless grasslands were wild and unenclosed.

Add to that the temptation to make up for losses in livestock and women by raiding other communities and we start to see why the steppe was an inherently unstable political environment. The nomadic-pastoralist lifestyle at its best could only meet the most basic needs of subsistence. For anything extra, or any luxuries, communities had to look elsewhere. Raiding was an essential and integral aspect of steppe life.

The steppe nomads were a nuisance to one another, but a terror to the settled peoples to the south and west of the steppe, whose communities they would attack from time to time. The farming folk had no real answer to the ferocity of the steppe warriors, nor to the astonishing equestrian skills that went with the nomadic lifestyle; the precision with which they could send arrows whizzing from their short bows at a gallop, wheeling and turning in an instant. The histories of the great civilizations of East Asia, India, Persia, the Middle East, the Mediterranean and Western Europe have all been profoundly affected by the invasions of steppe nomads of one sort or another. They have included the Indo-Aryans and the Hsiung-nu or Huns, as well as the Mongols and Turks of more recent times.

SCYTHIAN UNCERTAINTIES

The Scythians of the first millennium BCE herded and raided their way back and forth across much of what would one day be Russia long before the idea of any such place existed. Where the Scythians themselves thought they were is not clear. There does not seem to have been any 'Scythia', as such, only the people, the Scyths (as archaeologists used to call them) themselves.

This makes sense, given their existence on the move. Nomads necessarily travel light, both physically and culturally. They cannot afford to carry extensive archives with them (like the Scythians, they tend to be illiterate) and their connection with the land, although close, is not deep-rooted. We have no real way of knowing where or when the Scythians originated; they appeared in history only when they collided with established civilizations.

Several of the great empires found it easier to make deals with the Scythians than defeat them. Esarhaddon of Assyria may have given one of his daughters in marriage to Bartatua, one nomad leader, around 670 BCE. A generation later, taking advantage of the power vacuum left by the collapse of the Assyrian civilization, Bartatua's son, Madyes, led his bands against the Median kingdom of north-western Iran. He then pushed westward into Asia Minor before shifting direction south into Syria and Palestine – the Scythians making a brief appearance in the biblical narrative under the name of the *Ashkenaz*.

Below: A Scythian archer in the service of the Persians, this proud warrior was painted by the Greek artist Epiktetos in around 520 BCE.

Ultimately, they reached the borders of the Egyptian Empire. They could have ventured further, but allowed themselves to be bought off by the Pharaoh Psamtik I; as invaders, they were less concerned with glory than with plunder.

AN ELUSIVE ENEMY

The Scythians' pragmatism was reflected in their reactions in 514 BCE, when Darius I of Persia decided they were an irritation he would no longer tolerate. He marched an enormous army – said to have been 700,000 strong – across the Danube over pontoon bridges and out on to the steppe. Over and over again, reports the Greek historian Herodotus, Darius challenged the Scythians to do battle, but they simply withdrew.

Below: Scythian envoys observe the diplomatic niceties with the Emperor Darius, in this 19th-century representation. On the ground, they didn't need to fear Persian power.

The Scythians had no cities or infrastructure to defend – not even any fields. With nothing to prove by engaging such an overwhelming force, they vanished away into the steppe. Darius' army was chasing a chimera. Worse, it was being harried in its flanks and in its rear; having melted away, the Scythians reappeared when least expected, making incessant small-scale attacks that became draining. Darius' forces were demoralized, and badly depleted. They were fortunate to escape annihilation.

NO MAN'S LAND

The Scythians had their day soon enough. In the third century BCE, another group of nomads started pushing southwest into Scythian territory. The Sarmatians originated in lands to the north and east of Scythian territory, but were themselves dislodged by commotions further out on the steppe. As they were driven further westward, they encroached on the lands of the Scythians, pushing them further westward in their turn. Finally running out of room to manoeuvre, the Scythians were subjected by the Sarmatians and absorbed into their own tribal groups. The Scythians disappeared from history as abruptly as they had entered it – here and gone in the space of a few hundred years.

This was to be the case with the Sarmatians too: in the fourth century CE, another group of nomadic pastoralists, the Huns, started pushing westward out of Central Asia. They too were to roam and raid across much of Russia (and many other countries too). Like the Scythians and Sarmatians before them, they may have had a shocking impact on their first arrival, but they left little trace in history. They too registered only where they clashed with settled and civilized communities that went in for record keeping – hence their villain's role in the great drama of the Fall of Rome.

After the Huns came the Avars. Again, their exact origins are obscure, but if the Eurasian grassland was an 'ocean', these westward expansions were their tides.

As for the steppe itself, that was just the mysterious space they seemed to have emerged out of, and that's the impression we've been left with of the Russian grasslands of that time as well.

Above: The downward-curving quillon (crossguard) is characteristic of the sword used by the Scythians. Here it's extravagantly echoed in the curling pommel ornaments.

SKULLS, SKINS AND SCYTHIANS

THE MOST SUSTAINED and detailed description we have of the Scythians and their way of life comes from the Greek writer Herodotus, whose *Histories* appeared in 440 BCE. It is not clear how much of his report is first-hand, and how much was hearsay, although he is known to have visited some of the Greek trading colonies on the Black Sea's northern shores and may have forayed inland on to the steppe from there.

Herodotus wrote of the Scythians as a self-consciously 'civilized' Greek would write of a 'barbarian' enemy, and his testimony should be read with that in mind. However, as sensationalist as it might appear, his account is not considered too far-fetched by modern experts. Although the archaeological evidence relating to the Scythians is scant, neither this nor what we have learned of other nomadic pastoralist peoples seems wildly inconsistent with what Herodotus recorded:

As far as fighting is concerned, their customs are as follows: the Scythian warrior drinks the blood of the first enemy he overcomes in battle. However many he kills, he cuts off all their heads to take them to the king, given that he is entitled to a share of the booty, but this is forfeit if he can't produce a head. To strip the skin from the skull, he first makes an

Above: Two warriors fight it out in a field of gold in this stunning scene from the 4th century BCE.

incision around the head above the ears, then, seizing hold of the scalp, he shakes the skull out forcefully. After this, with an ox's rib, he scrapes the scalp clean of flesh, before softening it by rubbing it between his hands. From that time on, he can use it as a napkin. The Scyth is proud of these scalp-napkins, and hangs them from his bridle-rein; the more a man can show, the more highly he is esteemed. Many make themselves cloaks, like our peasants' sheepskins, by sewing considerable numbers of scalps together. Others flay the right arms of their dead enemies, and make of the skin, which is stripped off with the nails hanging to it, a covering for their quivers.

It was no man's land, much travelled and ferociously fought over, but ultimately never settled and never truly 'owned'.

WAVE THEORY

No one knows for sure whether the *Sclaveni* or Slavs who spilled across the steppe and on into the Balkans in the course of the 6th century CE represented another tide or were the human flotsam that it pushed before it. There is evidence that many of these migrants came on to the Russian plains from further west, in what is now Poland, or from the Carpathian Mountains further south. They were probably the descendants of earlier invaders, from the Scythian era through to more recent times, who had settled in Eastern Europe before being dislodged and dispersed by the arrival of the Avars.

Whatever their origins, the Slavs were soon settled across a wide area of Eastern Europe extending most of the way from the

Below: Trade – in slaves and other commodities – opened up the East European interior. Sergey Ivanov (1854–1910) captures the colour of what could be a very cruel commerce.

Baltic to the Balkans. They seem to have formed small village communities under local chiefs. Hunting in the forests, fishing in the rivers and streams, they also seem to have done a little farming, albeit on a very small and local scale. These seem to have been peaceful communities, presumably ill-equipped to deal with a new wave of arrivals in the 9th century, this time out of the north: the Vikings.

VIKINGS WITH A DIFFERENCE

'From the fury of the Northmen, may the Lord deliver us,' the monks of England's Northumbria prayed. God did not appear to have been listening when, in 793, according to the *Anglo-Saxon Chronicle*, 'the ravages of heathen men miserably destroyed God's church on Lindisfarne, with plunder and slaughter.' Raiding groups from Scandinavia spread panic and terror wherever they went round western Europe's coasts. These Norwegian and Danish Vikings had their counterparts in Sweden. They pushed south and eastward, crossing the Baltic Sea, making their way through Finland and up the Russian river system. As well as 'plunder and slaughter', however, they brought trade.

There is a straightforward explanation for this. With so little in the way of a civilized infrastructure – no rich monasteries, no cities, so no treasuries or palaces – there was little here that a raider could seize and carry off. Major monastic and civic

Below: In the West, as here on Britain's isle of Lindisfarne, the Vikings were known as wild raiders. In early Russia, there was more nuance to their role.

foundations in the west had accumulated treasures: gold and silver; gems and jewellery; fine fabrics; illuminated books and leatherwork. But the wealth of this vast and as yet largely unexploited region was growing in the fields – or, more often, running in the forests, for the richest product it had to offer were its furs.

THE RISE OF RUS

Just as, 800 years later, the English traders of King Charles II's Hudson's Bay Company started making their way through Canada's interior offering European products in return for pelts, so the Swedish Vikings plied the rivers of western Russia. They too would find it made sense to establish semi-permanent trading posts; over time, these often took root and grew very slowly into

Above: Councillors convene in the city of Veliky Novgorod, a trading centre by the 9th century and soon to be Russia's first great city.

cities. Pskov and Novgorod are both believed to have started out as riverbank bases for trade between Scandinavian Viking merchants and the Russian natives, as did Polotsk, in Belarus, and Chernihiv in Ukraine.

The Finns called the Vikings *Ruotsi*, or 'oarsmen'; the Slavic term *Rus* seems to have come from this. By any name, they were overbearing trading partners; their relationship with the tribes around the Baltic and, further south, in Slavic territories, was no more equal than that between Native Americans and Europeans. The Vikings did exchange goods with the wealthy chiefs they met, but they also appear to have raided defenceless villages and extorted furs from riverside communities. Hiring themselves out to the wealthier chiefs as 'Varangian' mercenaries, they involved themselves in local disputes, and soon made themselves an inseparable part of the Slavic scene.

The differences between the Rus and the Slavs began blurring over generations as a new Scandinavian–Slavic hybrid culture began to emerge. Among its most important centres were the towns of Ladoga, on Lake Ladoga, and Novgorod to the south of it, where a mixed population of Slavs, Finns and Scandinavians lived. As time went on and the Vikings' field of operations broadened, further settlements sprang up. The chief of these was down the River Dnieper in what is now Ukraine but at this time lay in the territory of the Slavic Polan people.

A VIKING FUNERAL

IN AROUND 920, AHMAD ibn-Fadlan wrote his *Risala* ('letter' or 'account'), describing a diplomatic mission he had made from Baghdad to the Volga valley. It includes the most detailed description ever recorded of the rituals surrounding the ship burial of a Viking chief:

The dead chieftain was put in a temporary grave which was covered for ten days until they had sewn new clothes for him. One of his slavewomen volunteered to join him in the afterlife and she was guarded day and night, being given a great amount of intoxicating drinks while she sang happily. When the time had arrived for cremation, they pulled his longship ashore and put it on a platform of wood, and they made a bed for the dead chieftain on the ship. Thereafter, an old woman referred to as the 'Angel of Death' put cushions on the bed. She was responsible for the ritual. Then they disinterred the
chieftain and gave him new clothes. ...The chieftain was put into his bed with all his weapons and grave offerings around him...

Meanwhile, the slave girl went from one tent to the other and had sexual intercourse with the men. Every man told her 'tell your master that I did this because of my love to him'...Then the slave girl was taken away to the ship. She...received several vessels of intoxicating drinks and she sang and bade her friends farewell.

Then the girl was pulled into the tent and the men started to beat on the shields so her screams could not be heard. Six men entered into the tent to have intercourse with the girl, after which they put her onto her master's bed. Two men grabbed her hands and two men her wrists. The angel of death put a rope around her neck and while two men pulled the rope, the old woman stabbed the girl between her ribs with a knife. Thereafter, the relatives of the

RURIK'S REIGN

Already the site of a small fortified settlement, Kiev had by tradition been founded by the brothers of the local Polan prince, Kij, and named in his honour. According to the *Chronicle of Nestor* (1113), it was under the rule of Khazar nomads when the mid-9th century brought a sudden change. Around 862, Slavs and Finns living in northwest Russia asked one of the Rus, a warrior named Rurik, to be their new prince. He based himself in Novgorod, from where his followers ventured southward, eventually establishing a new headquarters in Kiev.

'They assembled many Varangians around them,' says the

dead chieftain arrived with a burning torch and set the ship aflame...

Afterwards, a round barrow was built over the ashes and in the centre of the mound they erected a staff of birch wood, where they carved the names of the dead chieftain and his king. Then they departed in their ships.

Above: The elements of fire and water came together in the Viking ship-cremation.

Chronicle, 'and began to rule over the land of the Polans.' Later, Rurik's successor, Oleg, took personal charge in Kiev, which meant that the two most important cities in the region were in the control of Rurikid rulers.

This story might belong to the realm of myth rather than history; the name 'Rurikid' could be a back formation from the name of the kingdom, Rus. But Rus did seem to have an important part to play in Kiev's foundation. Over time, as the various Viking settlements in the corridor between the Baltic and the Black Sea started to coalesce into something like a state, this city became its de facto capital. Hence the name by which this first proto-Russian polity has passed into history: Kievan Rus.

The moment at which a loose alliance of adventurers can be seen as a state is not easy to identify, but at some point posterity decided that Kiev's ruling warlords could be referred to as 'grand princes'. Whatever we call them, they extended their area of

Below: Rurik and his brothers arrive at Staraya Ladoga for the trading-stop which would one day make history, as imagined by Viktor Vasnetsov (1848–1926).

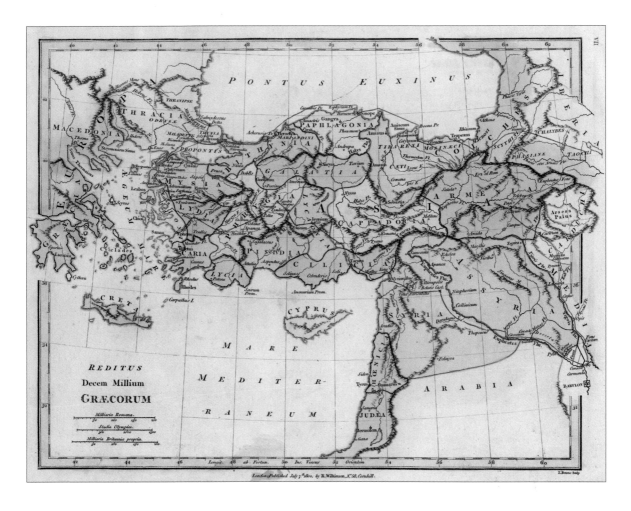

influence across vast areas of Russia, trading with (or extorting tribute from) the remoter Slavic tribes.

BYZANTINE COMPLEXITIES

The flow of Scandinavian Varangian mercenaries downriver went on unabated, and Kiev grew in power as well as size. Its increasing wealth and influence in the region as a whole brought it into contact with southwest Asia's superpower: the Byzantine Empire. This great state was centred on the Bosphorus and the city of Constantinople – which, since its later conquest by the Turks, we've known as Istanbul. The Roman Emperor Constantine (reigned 306–37 CE) had renamed the former Greek colony of Byzantium in his own honour, establishing his imperial capital there. Rome itself, under repeated barbarian attack, had been in

Above: Through the early Middle Ages, the Byzantine Empire – shown here in a map of 1800 – extended over much of the Near East.

decline during this period, clearing the way for Constantinople to become the great metropolis of the first millennium.

Although the Byzantines saw their empire as still essentially 'Roman' (their Arab enemies continued to call them the *Rom*), it was not the same militaristic state that had built the classic 'Roman Empire'. Byzantine power was primarily economic; its expansionism was mercantile, and for the most part directed eastward into Asia. Like the old Rome, though, the Byzantine Empire saw itself as the world's pre-eminent power – and its policeman.

THERE WAS NOT MUCH SIGN OF ANYONE IN RUS'S RULING HOUSE LEARNING TO LOVE THEIR NEIGHBOURS AS THEMSELVES.

The first Vikings to make it as far as Constantinople had called it Miklagard, 'the great city'. The Rus of Kiev came to call it Zargrad. This was a Slavic name, *grad* or *gorod* meaning 'city'; *zar* or *czar* their contraction of the Latin *caesar*, for 'emperor'. For them, it was a source of desirable luxuries, such as the silks and jewellery, which they bought with furs and slaves. (The modern English word 'slave' dates back to the many thousands of 'Slavs' the Byzantines bought from the Kievan traders at this time.)

CHRISTIAN SOLDIERS

These contacts were not always peaceable, and fleets of longships attacked Constantinople a number of times – most notably in 860, in response to attempts by the Byzantine authorities to strike a trade deal advantageous to the Khazars. These were Turkic nomadic people who had mostly put their raiding ways behind them, but in the process had established themselves as trading rivals to the Vikings in this part of southwest Asia. The Vikings would not take this lying down. For Kievan Rus, mercantilism and militarism were two sides of the same coin.

Sometimes these Viking warriors sold their skills as mercenaries. The Byzantines certainly appreciated their warlike capabilities: many Varangians were taken into their service from the late 9th century on. The connection was institutionalized in 988: in return for the hand of Anna (953–1011), sister of

Emperor Romanos II (reigned 959–63). Grand Prince Vladimir the Great (reigned 969–77) sent 6000 men to Constantinople to became the core of a permanent Imperial Varangian Guard. Devoutly Orthodox – and, it seems, an eager proselytizer in her new homeland, starting with her husband – Grand Princess Anna personifies an already developing identification on the part of Kievan Rus with a wider Christendom. Continuing commerce, and mercenary service, continued to strengthen these important bonds.

Above: No longer raiders but, taken on to form the Emperor's 'Varangian Guard', Viking warriors became a bastion of the Byzantine state.

SUCCESSION STRUGGLES

There was not much sign of anyone in Rus's ruling house learning to love their neighbours as themselves; they could just about tolerate each other. Vladimir had only come to the throne after an epic succession struggle with his half-brothers, Yaropolk and Oleg. As an illegitimate son, he was just a spectator at this stage. As his siblings had embarked upon a

Above: Grand Prince Yaropolk falls dead, killed by his half-brother Vladimir – back from his Swedish exile with his supporters to seize the throne.

full-scale civil war, and Oleg was killed in 976, Vladimir was a spectator from a safe distance, having fled north to Scandinavia to find refuge. In 980, however, Vladimir came home with an army of Swedish Vikings, defeated and killed Yaropolk and appointed himself grand prince.

When Vladimir died in 1015, Yaropolk's son seized power. Posterity left little doubt as to how it saw his accession, naming him 'Sviatopolk the Accursed' while canonizing Vladimir's older sons, St Boris and St Gleb, both of whom Sviatopolk killed, along with a younger brother, Sviatoslav.

But things were more complicated, the *Chronicles* agreed. Sviatopolk had some claim to have been Vladimir's oldest son: Kievan Rus's first Christian ruler, having killed his brother, had raped his widow.

'Christian' values change with time, of course, but it is hard to think of a period when Sviatopolk I (*c*.980–1019; reigned 1015–19) would have passed muster. He spent his four-year reign fighting off the challenge of Vladimir's youngest son, Yaroslav; he was finally defeated and died in his turn.

Kiev reached its zenith under Grand Prince Yaroslav the Wise. He enlarged and beautified the city and enhanced its reputation. He maintained diplomatic relations not just with the Byzantine Empire but with the rulers of Scandinavia, the German Empire, Poland, Bohemia, Hungary and France. He was also a warrior, in 1036 winning a glorious victory over the Pechenegs, the latest wave of Turkic raiders from the Central Asian Steppe.

MONGOL MENACE

If the defeat of the Pechenegs was good news, the need to fight them in the first place was an unwelcome reminder of the seemingly endless trouble that had come out of the steppe in centuries past. The rise of Kievan Rus had seemingly stemmed this flow – and for a couple of hundred years it would continue to – but it would begin again with Genghis Khan.

'Genghis Khan' is a title, not a name: it means, roughly, 'Very Mighty King'. The man who bore it was born Temujin (*c.* 1165–1227), the son of Yesugei, a minor chieftain. Yesugei died when Temujin was young; without his protection, his son was ostracized. Temujin learned to stand up for himself. He gathered

SAVED BY ST GEORGE?

EARLY MEDIEVAL CHRONICLERS took a comparatively relaxed approach to timelines in their works; they were more concerned with symbolic resonances and moral meanings than mere facts. So we don't know with any certainty when a sizeable crew of Varangians arrived in Paphlagonia, part of what is now northern Turkey's Black Sea coastal strip, and descended on the city of Amastris (now Amasra). Scholars now believe this was some time in the 830s or 40s, although the way the author of the *Life of St George of Amastris* tells the story, it seems pedantic to fuss about dates too much. Far more important to him is the pagan savagery of the 'barbarians of Rus, a people who as everyone knows are cruel and unkind and show no mercy to people, regardless of rank or age.'

Fortunately for the people of the city – and, in a higher, more spiritual scheme – for the pagan attackers, Saint George – despite having been dead for the best part of half a century and interred in the crypt of a church in Amastris. The Vikings, it seems, burst into his chapel to start stripping it of gold and jewels, but, just as they were about to start on the saint's tomb, they were suddenly struck into paralysis and could not move or speak. Awed by this intervention from God, it is said, the Varangians converted to Christianity.

It was from around this time that Kievan Rus started embracing the Orthodox creed, although whether their conversion was miraculous or more mundane is a matter for conjecture. A more sceptical view might see it as the natural consequence of generations of cultural contact; a more cynical one as a pragmatic, even commercial, calculation.

OF WASPS AND WARRIORS

THE VIKING ATTACK ON **Constantinople** on 18 June 860 was as frightening as it was fast and furious: 200 longships appeared out of nowhere. For the Orthodox Patriarch, Photios I, it was 'a thunderbolt from heaven'. The Vikings wrought havoc by sacking monasteries, slaughtering people and burning houses. The Byzantines were badly placed for self-defence: much of their army was in Asia Minor fending off an Arab attack, and their naval forces were fighting the Normans in the Aegean Sea.

The Vikings did not manage to menace Constantinople proper: that city remained safe behind its fortifications. Perhaps, then, Photios' comment that the raiders came on like 'a swarm of wasps' was a double-edged description: does it mean that the Kievan onslaught was more of a nuisance than a menace? Maybe. However, Photios was quick to see the Vikings' withdrawal after some six weeks' siege as a miraculous, divinely ordained deliverance.

Above: The Viking raid on Byzantium, featured in the 15th-century *Radziwill Chronicle*.

a group of young fighters around him, drawn by his charisma, and impressed by his abilities in battle. By 1206, he had won his title as Khan of all the Mongols, forging a united people out of an array of squabbling tribes. He had also created a spectacularly successful war machine, as the peoples of China, India, the Middle East and Europe were to find.

He hardly had to train his warriors in archery and close-quarters fighting, but he made sure that they practised daily to hone their skills. Mounted manoeuvring was an essential part of herding and hunting life, but there was always scope to iron out imperfections. Many of his troops fought as armoured lancers; Genghis Khan developed mounted manoeuvres for these men, drilling them tirelessly until they were second nature. Mongol troops travelled light. Most had only layers of seasoned leather by way of armour; the lancers' would be stiffened with plates of iron or bone. Agility in the saddle kept them safe for the most part; their little horses' stamina and speed was a secret weapon. Settled peoples, hearing of Mongol attacks some distance off, invariably underestimated how quickly the invaders would arrive.

FULL GALLOP

The Mongol troops swept like a storm through eastern Asia, invading northwestern China in 1207. They sacked Beijing in 1215, before heading south into the heartland of the Middle Kingdom. Moving west, they attacked the cities of the Central Asian Silk Road. The pace of their progress was dizzying, yet there was much more to them than élan. Genghis Khan had been developing and improving his fighting force. Wherever he had gone, along with his other plunder, he had taken capture talent: weapons-makers, armourers and, above all, engineers. This most mobile of armies had become a world-beater in the most static form of warfare: the Mongols were renowned for their skill in siegecraft.

The Mongols could fill the deepest moats at speed with sandbags; their giant catapults could hurl anything, from flaming naphtha to putrid animal carcasses, over the highest battlements; they had engines that could shoot dozens of fire-arrows at a time. They also had another weapon: that of sheer terror, which Genghis Khan was never shy of using when required. When Samarkand fell after a siege in 1220, the Mongol leader had its

Below: An improbable imperialist, Genghis Khan made a virtue of his warriors' lightweight weaponry, their mobility and speed to build one of the greatest empires ever seen.

'ASIAN' CRUELTY

THE VIEW THAT THERE is an 'Asiatic' streak in the national character that makes Russians prone to cruelty may seem nonsensical now, but didn't always. Lent a certain superficial credibility by the succession of invasions by steppe nomads (who were wild and, in many cases, cruel), this view flourished among even comparatively respectable historians and demographers in the late 19th century; this was the height of Race Theory in the West.

After World War II, the Cold War brought new ideological imperatives in the West: from the 1950s on it became important to play down the heroism of the Russians' defence of their country during the 'Great Patriotic War'. Their stoic resistance under German attack was recast as a barely human insensitivity, just as the savagery of the Red Army's attack on Germany as the tide turned in the war was presented as two sides of the same coin. The idea of the inscrutably mysterious and implacably cruel 'Asiatic' Russian was built up as a semi-mythic threat.

Killing and cruelty were part of the Russian story from the start, and as European as

the *Ruotsi* were. Consider, for example, the fate of Anastasia, mistress of Prince Yaroslav Osmomysl (*c*.1135–87), when her lover decided to leave his wife for her. His *boyars* (leading nobles), concerned at the influence this woman might wield over their lord, abducted her and burned her at the stake. And if Batu Khan's sack of Kiev in 1240 was to leave the city a devastated wasteland, earlier attacks by the other up-and-coming cities of Rus through the 12th century would have run it close. In 1169, the forces of Sviatoslav Vsevolodovich (d. 1194) left the city a smoking ruin; in 1174, they came back to rampage through the city for 12 days straight. In 1203, it was the turn of Rurik Rostislavich (d. 1215) and his Polovtsian allies. There is little evidence of either kinship sympathy or Christian compassion between Russian rivals.

Right: It's hard to see which side is the more 'savage' in this scene of Russian carnage as European Vikings engage with Turkic Pecheneg raiders.

inhabitants slaughtered and their skulls arranged into a pyramid as a warning to other peoples who might be tempted to resist.

By 1222, the Mongols were making a diversion into northern India. The following year, they made their first foray on to the southern Russian steppe. A coalition force came out to meet them, under the command of Prince Mstislav III of Kiev. His army was backed not only by soldiers from Smolensk and other Slavic states but Turkic Cuman warbands, who could see the writing on the wall for their power on the western steppe.

Towards the end of May, on the plains east of the Dnieper, the two forces met, the Mongols under the command of two of Genghis Khan's most skilled and seasoned generals, Jebe (d. 1223) and Subotai (1175–1248). The Russians fared better than had been feared, eventually putting the Mongol invaders to flight. However, as the Russians pursued their 'defeated' enemy in the following days, they broke formation and became more and more stretched out. When the Mongols paused by Ukraine's Kalka River, turned, formed for battle and charged

Above: Genghis Khan leads his warriors into China: even the strongest settled empires found it impossible to defend against the Mongols' mobility, speed and sheer ferocity.

Above: Genghis Khan's son and successor, Ogedei Khan invaded Rus in 1237, his forces spreading terror and devastation wherever they went.

their pursuers, the Russians were pretty much scythed down in their path.

Having defeated the Rus by means of a cunning tactical retreat, the Mongols spared them with a strategic retreat, abruptly abandoning the battlefield, wheeling away and withdrawing back into the vastness of the steppe.

BACK WITH A VENGEANCE

What occasioned the Mongol's abrupt about-turn is not known: that it was not due to clemency became clear when they returned, under the command of Genghis Khan's son Ogedei (1186–1241), 14 years later. His forces invaded Russia in 1237, leaving a trail of devastation. Up to 50 per cent of the population of Rus is believed to have been killed by the advancing Mongols, and what had shown signs of being the beginnings of a more modern urban culture was erased.

The capital, Kiev, was especially hard hit: it was taken in 1240 by an army led by Batu Khan (1205–55). Impressed by the city's splendour, say the chroniclers, the Mongol general sent envoys offering to spare it. Showing more daring than discretion, the

BLOODLESS BRUTALITY

MSTISLAV III AND HIS aristocratic entourage were spared the fate of their more lowly followers, thanks to a Mongol taboo on the shedding of noble blood. However, if they thought they would be let off lightly, they were quickly and cruelly disabused of the notion. Their conquerors had a wooden dais built on which to drink, eat and dance to celebrate their victory. This was placed on top of the bound but living bodies of their defeated foes. The victory banquet went ahead over the gasping, choking, suffocating and dying princes, the Mongols' dancing feet driving home their disdain for Rus's rulers.

Kievans put his delegation to the sword. Batu Khan brought up catapults and other siege engines and, after a three-day assault, his forces found their way into the city, embarking on a spree of violence and plunder. Out of a population of 50,000, it is reported, only 2000 survived.

It is often assumed that statistics like this are mythic and massively exaggerated. We don't have reliable records, and this sort of slaughter does seem (literally) overkill, but that may have made sense as policy. However redoubtable their martial skills, the Mongols' secret weapon was the wave of shock and awe – and sheer terror – that preceded them, prompting many cities to submit before a single arrow had been shot.

Ogedei's armies continued westwards, with separate warbands making exploratory forays into Poland and Hungary. On 9 April 1241, at Legnica or Liegnitz in Poland, a small subsidiary force led by Subotai smashed a Silesian army. Two days later, the Mongols' main force defeated the Hungarians at Mohi. The way to western Europe, with all its riches, was wide open.

Then from the east came the news that Ogedei Khan had died. All the Mongol chiefs were called back for a conclave to elect his successor. By the time his successor, Guyuk Khan (c.1206–48) was in place, the Mongols were preoccupied with other campaigns in the eastern regions of their realm. But the southern grassland regions of Kievan Rus lay well within the Mongol Empire. The northern forests still had some

Below: In 1222, Kiev's Mstislav III had held back the initial advance of the Mongols. Over time, though, they were to prove irresistible.

autonomy, but its Russian rulers still paid tribute to the Khans. The empire as a whole broke up from the edges inwards over the generations that followed, but a residual policy, known as the 'Golden Horde', remained. This stretched from Central into western Asia, and much of southern Russia lay along its margins. It lasted into the 16th century, largely in peace, despite the carnage in which it had been created.

> **'THEY MURDERED SO MANY OF THE UNBAPTIZED THAT MANY DROWNED IN THEIR OWN BLOOD.'**

AN ANTI-CHRISTIAN CRUSADE
As if a pagan enemy from the east was not enough, in the early decades of the 13th century the northern Russian principalities had to contend with a Christian foe from further west. The Teutonic Knights, a German order of military priests, had been founded in the Middle East at the time of the Third Crusade (1189–92). Since then, they had found a new role in the north, suppressing the pagan tribes of eastern Prussia, Livonia and Lithuania. 'They murdered so many of the unbaptized that many drowned in their own blood,' the chronicler Nicholas von Jeroschin recorded.

By the 1230s, the Teutonic Knights had decided to widen their own remit, campaigning not only against Prussian pagans but against the Orthodox Christians of Russia. Attacking Novgorod

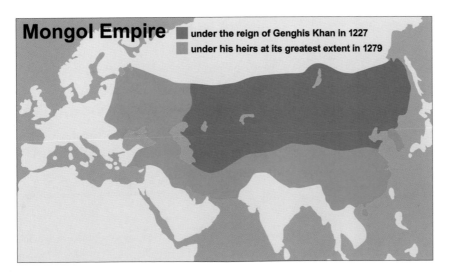

Mongol Empire ■ under the reign of Genghis Khan in 1227
■ under his heirs at its greatest extent in 1279

Opposite: Conquering Mongols hold aloft the head of Silesia's Henry II, 1241, in an illustration from a 15th-century chronicle.

Left: Already vast by the death of Genghis Khan in 1227, the Mongol Empire was to grow even larger under his successors.

in 1240, they were badly defeated two years later by Prince Alexander Nevsky (1221–63) at the famous Battle of the Ice. Allowing themselves to be drawn out on to the frozen surface of Lake Peipus by Alexander's tactical retreat, the heavily armoured knights found their horses struggling to keep their footing. Repelled by a resolute Russian infantry, they became a sitting target for Alexander's archers. Much later, in the Soviet era, this inspired Russian patriotism in the face of a renewed Teutonic threat, in *Alexander Nevsky,* Sergei Eisenstein's film of 1938.

RUSSIA REBORN

'They make a wasteland and call it peace,' the Roman historian Tacitus had claimed of his countrymen in their imperial expansionism. The same might be said for the Mongols' legacy in Russia. Further east, the heartlands of the Golden Horde enjoyed prosperity, but the Russian territories represented an impoverished western fringe. Further north, moreover, in those nominally autonomous principalities that remained 'Russian' but struggled to assert themselves or haul themselves out of the slough in which they were enmired, economic and political life went on – but at a very low wattage.

So things trundled on for a century or so. Not until the 1350s did any signs of new life stir. Under Dmitry Donskoy (1350–89), Moscow came to the fore in the endless but previously inconclusive jostling and bickering between the Russian realms and mounted the first serious pushback against the power of the Golden Horde. Its only real rival now was Novgorod.

With his victory over the Mongols at the Battle of Kulikovo (1380), Donskoy gave himself and Moscow a moral edge in the tussle for ascendancy within Rus. The accession in 1462 of Ivan III (1440–1505; 'the Great') as Grand Prince of Moscow quickly led to Moscow's accession as the grand principality of Rus. Ivan the Great did more than anyone to craft the country we know as Russia – for worse as well as for better. In asserting Russian pride, he shut out the Catholic Church – and, maybe more damagingly, the Western European culture which came with it. Russia arguably owes its insularity, as well as its independence, to Ivan's reign.

IN TATARS

As the Mongols made their way westward, they formed alliances with other, mainly Turkic, nomad groups. These became known in Russian history collectively as Tatars. Although in lifestyle and warlike ways they were not that different from the Mongols, they had their own separate history and, as time went on, they would diverge again. It was largely the Tatars who, after the withdrawal of the Mongols in the 13th century, remained in control of the Central Asian Golden Horde. Over the centuries that followed, this would slowly disintegrate into separate Khanates.

For the most part, the Tatars were not much of a threat to Russia, although they did go raiding from time to time. They did represent an alien 'other', though, not least because, from the 14th century, most Tatars were committed converts to Sunni Islam.

One of the most important legacies the Tatars left on Russian history was indirect. Peasants dislodged by raids in the south and east flocked north and settled on the lands of wealthy nobles. At first they squatted. When their status was officially recognized, from the 16th century on, it was as serfs, bound to local landowners by feudal ties.

Above: Russian forces fight off Tatar raiders in a painting by an unknown artist (1901).

2

LIFE, DEATH AND TYRANNY

Ivan IV Vasilyevich was the first Russian ruler to give himself the title 'Czar', but he was a prototype in other, more disturbing, ways.

SEVERAL FRIENDS and acquaintances recall the playwright Anton Chekhov making the aesthetic argument that would become known as 'Chekhov's gun'. It called for a dramatic style that was stripped down and spare, in which 'everything that has no relevance' should be removed. 'One must never place a loaded rifle on the stage if it isn't going to be fired,' Chekhov said.

Chekhov's choice of image is significant: why a rifle rather than a rose, a book, a candle or a pair of shoes? All decent drama should ultimately be about questions of life and death importance, maybe, but does it have to involve literal life and death? The same might be said of the Russian story: beside the milder, more nuanced, histories of other countries, it seems a stark narrative, high in violence and shock. Essential to that austerity has been an attitude to authority for which it has seemed that, as though in a political equivalent of Chekhov's gun, power isn't power if it isn't used. Repeatedly in Russian

Opposite: 'Terrible' indeed, Ivan IV established a dreadful template for royal authority in Russia: despotic, ruthless, paranoid, cruel and capricious.

history, we find freedom giving way to authoritarianism, and authoritarianism tending towards tyranny.

IMAGINED OFFENCES?

At times, this tyranny has been attended by insane paranoia. What else could explain the reaction of Ivan IV (*c.*1530–84) to the 'Novgorod Treason' of 1569? What this 'treason' consisted of was never clear. Had Ivan been angered by reports that the city's ruling council had been thinking of secession, that Novgorod might leave Russia to join neighbouring Lithuania (itself just joined with Poland in the Union of Lublin)? Was he sending out a message to other independent-minded cities? Or was it just that the wealth, sophistication and civic self-confidence of this trading centre on the Volkhov River affronted a dour and suspicious Ivan Vasilyevich who had never been slow to explode into a rage?

Whatever the provocation, his reaction was overwhelming, as a chronicle of the period makes clear. The Czar, it says, had 'the powerful boyars, the important merchants, the administrative officials, and the citizens of every rank...brought before him, together with their wives and children', and ordered that they be tortured in 'spiteful, horrible, and inhuman ways'. Then, the chronicler continues, Ivan:

ordered that their bodies be tormented and roasted with fire in refined ways. And the Czar commanded his nobles to bind the hands and feet and heads of these tortured and roasted human beings with fine ropes in various ways. He ordered that each man be tied to a sled, be dragged to the Volkhov

Below: The Soviet actor Nikolai Cherkasov brings the monstrous Czar to life in Sergei Eisenstein's celebrated film *Ivan the Terrible* (1945–6).

bridge behind the fast-moving sleds, and be thrown into the Volkhov River from the bridge. The Czar ordered that their wives and children be brought to the Volkhov bridge where a high platform had been erected. He commanded that they be chained on the arms and legs and that the children be tied to their mothers and then be thrown from the platform into the waters of the Volkhov River... When the people, men and women of all ages, surfaced, they were stabbed by the soldiers with hooks, lances, and spears, or they were struck with axes.

Ivan's lust for blood was only whetted by such spectacles. Chroniclers describe him personally running women through with a spear and hacking men's bodies into pieces with his sword. He had one man quartered 'like a goose, ready for roasting'.

Above: With hangings, beheadings and impalings being conducted all about him, Ivan the Terrible leads a line of captives to their execution in this woodcut.

CEREMONIAL SADISM

If Novgorod was punished cruelly for its mysterious transgression, more personal scores remained to be settled with its alleged agents at Ivan's own court. In a pattern that would

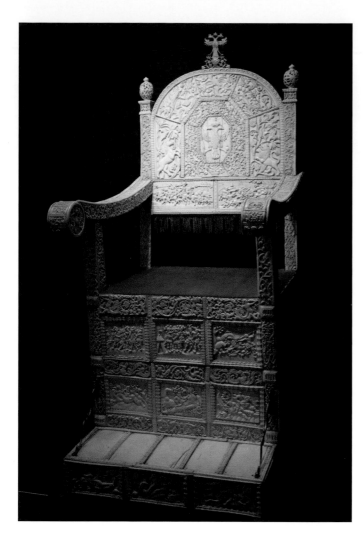

Above: As white as his deeds were black, Ivan the Terrible's ivory throne is still to be seen in the Armoury Museum of Moscow's Kremlin.

seem to foreshadow the Great Terror of Stalin, any boyar who was seen as a threat was detained and subjected to interrogation and torture until they had denounced others who would be tortured in their turn. Ivan was often present for these proceedings, and they were conducted with a creativity that suggests that this was as much a pleasure as a duty.

An eyewitness reports a ceremony held before a great crowd in Red Square, Moscow, with Ivan making his entrance with a thousand guards. Before them they drove 200 tortured nobles, many of them crawling, dragging broken legs behind them, and all bruised and bleeding from days and nights of brutal treatment. At first, the crowd was hushed, fearful of what they saw and anxious about why they had been summoned there. But Ivan spoke to them, reassuring them of their safety, and soon they were cheering as the spectacle started to unfold. One by one, the 'conspirators' were brought forward to be publicly humiliated.

Ivan's Keeper of the Seal and Foreign Minister, Ivan Mikhailovich Viskovati, was accused of conspiring not just with the Lithuanians but with the Turks. Strung up by the hands between two tall wooden stakes, he was whipped about the head and body before fellow courtiers cut off first his nose, then his ears and then his genitals. Over the following hours, he bled to death. Ivan's Treasurer, Nikita Funikov, came next: he was drenched by turns with pails of icy-cold and boiling water until he lost consciousness and died.

ENFANT TERRIBLE

If Ivan Vasilyevich lacked people skills, this is hardly to be
wondered at, given a background in which power and privilege
had gone together with severe trauma. He had begun his
apprenticeship in violent intrigue early, becoming the Grand
Prince of Moscow at the age of only three, following the death of
his father, Vasily III (1479–1533). Just five years later, his mother,
Elena Glinskaya (*c.*1510–38), who had been acting as his regent,
died (very likely poisoned), leaving him an orphan. The boyars
charged with his protection seem to have derided and neglected
him, at worst subjecting him to savage beatings. More damaging
if less perceptible, perhaps, was the psychological impact of being

Left: Though a ruthless
ruler by normal standards,
Ivan's father, Vassily III
(1479–1533; Grand Prince
of Moscow, 1505–33),
was a veritable saint
beside his son.

a boy whose very existence was resented by those around him; he had lost his mother only to gain a world of enemies.

Unsurprisingly, there was a price to be paid. First by the innocent pets he hurled from the highest towers of the Kremlin; he laughed to look down at their lifeless, shattered forms below. Later, as he grew older, and could cruise the streets of Moscow with a gang of boyar boys, by the poor and elderly pedestrians they bullied and the girls they raped and maybe murdered – some

A CARNIVAL OF CRUELTY

IT WAS A RUSSIAN, the philosopher and literary critic Mikhail Bakhtin (1895–1975), who first pointed to the radical political aspects of medieval and early-modern carnival, and of that wider 'carnivalesque' sensibility that he saw represented in such self-consciously vulgar writers as France's François Rabelais (c. 1490–1553). Carnival, he noted, up-ended the usual cultural hierarchies, making fun of high authority through caricature and catcall and elevating the 'low', allowing drunkenness, song, sexual licence and scatology (lavatory humour) to have free rein. What was normally held up as wisdom had to defer to folly at these festive times.

Ivan was unusual: even in Russia, few rulers have been so cruel. But he stands out in other, lesser, ways as well – ways that may be important in hinting at the sort of insecurities that drove his paranoia. Carnival, conventionally, was the blackly comic cry of the oppressed, so it is curious that Ivan claimed it for his own. In 1568,

for example, he had prosecuted a boyar, I.P. Fedorov, who he suspected of plotting against him, with a show trial in which he was the accused and the prisoner the 'judge'. He had Fedorov dressed in regal gowns and placed on his own Czar's throne, to be addressed with all the respect and ceremony due to a royal judge, while Ivan, at ground level, was arraigned as suspect. This lasted until the moment when, the painful pantomime over, he gave the order for Fedorov's execution.

Another moment of monstrous carnival came in Novgorod in 1570, when the city's Archbishop Pimen was arrested. Accused of having conspired to turn his Orthodox archdiocese over to (Catholic) Lithuania-Poland, he was told he had betrayed his priestly role so was now a layman. As such, his vow of celibacy no longer held – in token of which Ivan's henchmen conducted a mock marriage between the prelate and a mare, into whose saddle he was subsequently tied, facing backwards, and sent trotting ignominiously out of town.

were buried alive or fed to bears, it is said, so they couldn't reveal what had been done to them.

Still a child when he came to the throne, Ivan seemed set to be manipulated by the different factions of boyars at the Moscow court. In the event, he had his own ideas and astounding assurance – and ruthlessness – at putting them into practice. He was only 13 when he ordered his first assassination. Prince Andrei Shuisky, a long-term tormentor of young Ivan, was beaten to death at his command.

CZAR QUALITY

In 1547, still just 16, Ivan took power personally, becoming the first Russian ruler to adopt the title *Czar* (from the Roman 'Caesar'). His marriage to Anastasia Romanovna Zakharina (1530–60) soon after seems to have stabilized his life to some extent. He showed his capacity for effective action when, in 1552, he conquered the Tatar Khanate of Kazan. The following

Above: Ivan IV oversees the spit-roasting of a prisoner: there was a grimly comic quality to many of his atrocities.

Opposite: This forensic
facial reconstruction
of Marfa Sobakina has
an otherworldly pallor
appropriate to her death
just days into her marriage
with the Czar.

Below: Ivan's aspect isn't
so much terrible as regal
(and oddly Roman) in this
depiction of his Conquest
of Kazan, 1552, by Pyotr
Shamshin (1811–95).

year, in the aftermath of English navigator Richard Chancellor's discovery of the White Sea route, he reopened trade between Russia and the West. It had dwindled almost to nothing in his predecessors' reigns.

Ivan extended his kingdom again in 1556, taking another Tatar Khanate, Astrakhan, opening up the way to the Volga, the Caspian Sea, the Caucasus, and ultimately Siberia. In 1558, he attacked the Germanic Livonian Knights (a subsection of the Teutonic Knights) who restricted Russian access to the Baltic. This was to turn into a protracted war involving Sweden, northern Europe's leading power.

INTO INSANITY

Up to now, it might be said that Ivan's reign, although ruthlessly effective, had not strayed too far beyond the normal standards

of those tough times. No one held on to regal power for long in any country in early-modern Europe without being ready to see off rivals and squash conspiracies. After his wife Anastasia's death in 1560, however, Ivan's suspicions spiralled out of control. Paranoia became the determining characteristic of his rule. That this wasn't entirely unjustified only exacerbated the problem. Many around Ivan undoubtedly did fear, envy and hope to oust him. He was convinced that Anastasia had been poisoned – and traces of arsenic and mercury found in her bones since suggest he may have been right.

LEADING OFFICIALS AND CHURCHMEN WERE SO WORRIED ABOUT IVAN'S INSTABILITY THAT THEY MOUNTED A CAMPAIGN TO GET HIM TO REMARRY.

How far he had 'loved' his late wife we cannot know. We cannot know how far he could be said to have loved anyone, damaged as he had been by his childhood experiences. But he had certainly depended on Anastasia emotionally, and the want of a woman's touch seems to have sent him off the rails. Although he could supply his sexual needs – and did, in a life of untrammelled debauchery and sadism – he couldn't find a way through his deeper feelings of bereavement. On the contrary, this waywardness seems only to have underlined his sense of psychological disorientation and strengthened his suspicion of those around him. A pattern emerged of his pulling courtiers close, coming to depend on them, then fearing and resenting that dependency and finally denouncing them. A stream of former friends went to their deaths.

MARRIAGE AND MADNESS

Leading officials and churchmen were so worried about Ivan's instability that they mounted a campaign to get him to remarry. A year or so later, he married Maria Temryukovna (c.1544–69), disliked by both court and people (the latter believed she was a witch). She may have been disliked by her husband, too. When she

THE COSSACKS AND THE CZAR

ANOTHER OF IVAN'S ACHIEVEMENTS (or offences – their role in history was often to be controversial) was to bring the Cossacks into the service of the Russian state. These communities of horsemen and their families had grown up in the wilds of the western steppe, during the decline of the Golden Horde, at a time of mounting anarchy, when warlordism was rife, and mercenary soldiering a way of life.

For a long time, the Cossacks had served the various Tatar chieftains on a freelance basis, guarding headquarters, escorting caravans and conducting raids. Having captured Astrakhan in 1556, Ivan was loath to lose it again; he approached the Cossacks, offering them generous terms to turn their backs on the Tatars and come into his service. They were to spearhead his

expansion into Siberia and would protect successive Czars from that time on. As time went on and discontent and democratic aspirations grew, the Cossacks were resented as the brutal enforcers of reaction.

Right: The Cossacks are as mysterious in their origins as they are historically iconic.

died in 1569, he was widely suspected of having poisoned her – although, true to form, he had several courtiers executed for her 'murder'.

A bride show followed Maria's death: twelve young women were paraded before the Czar so he could make his choice. Marfa Sobakina (1552–69), a merchant's daughter from Novgorod, was chosen. Within a day or so of the wedding, she was sickening; within about a fortnight she was dead – almost certainly poisoned, although most likely accidentally, by a drug her mother had administered in hopes of boosting her fertility. Ivan, of course, was convinced that his enemies were closing in on him. A further wave of denunciations and executions followed.

A year later came a new wife, Anna Koltovskaya (d. 1626), although without the blessing of the Orthodox Church, which forbade fourth marriages. She couldn't give her husband an heir and was soon set aside. She was at least allowed to live, albeit in the confinement of a convent. Much the same happened to her successor, Anna Vasilchikova (d. *c.*1577). After her came Vasilisa Melentyeva (d. 1579), a beautiful widow. She is said to have been the wife Ivan loved most passionately, and the one who was most of a match for him emotionally. Her affair with a prince at court enraged him so much that he forced her to watch as her lover was impaled alive on a wooden stake. She was then shipped off to another convent.

She may have been followed by Maria Dolgorukaya (d. 1580); then again, she may not have been. Legend has it that Ivan

Below: A terrible Czar in a tender moment: Ivan watches by the bedside of Vasilisa Melentyeva, reputedly the most beloved of his wives.

drowned her after discovering on their first night that she was not a virgin. The official record makes no mention of her, so she may only be a figment of folklore. Ivan *is* known to have married Maria Nagaya (d. *c.*1608) in 1581. She bore the Czar a son, Dmitri.

That same year, Ivan was to lose another son: his second (and, since his elder brother's death in infancy, his eldest), Ivan Ivanovich. He killed his designated successor himself in a fit of rage. The two are said to have quarrelled after Czar Ivan boxed his daughter-in-law's ears for some breach of etiquette: his son upbraided him and he hit out at his head with the wooden staff he was carrying, causing fatal injuries.

FAVOURITE FYODOR

IVAN'S DEEPEST, MOST ENDURING, relationship after Anastasia's death appears to have been with Fyodor Basmanov – what previous, more prudish, historians would describe as a 'favourite' of Ivan's, but we might more frankly and accurately call his lover.

Allegations of homosexual activity at this time have to be treated with circumspection. Then as now, they were often made as a demeaning smear. All the same, the volume and consistency of the testimony tends to support the view that Ivan was bisexual. He was undoubtedly close to Basmanov. It is reported that Basmanov was effeminate in his personal presentation, although also a clever and heroically courageous military commander. Whether or not it is true that he would dress in women's clothes and dance seductively for the Czar's entertainment, he does appear to have lived for some time as Ivan's consort, sharing his bed.

Basmanov was ultimately to go the same way as previous companions: he was among those accused of plotting against him in Novgorod in 1570. He escaped execution with his co-conspirators only because he had already died in prison under torture.

DIVIDE AND RULE

The violent instability of the Czar's domestic life was reflected in Russia more widely in what amounted to a reign of terror. Even by the standards of an absolute ruler, Ivan seemed megalomaniacal in his tendency to play God with his subjects and his realm. In 1552, for instance, in taking the city of Kazan from the Tatars, his forces killed more than 65,000 people and expelled many thousands more. He did so in the name of faith, bringing in Christian settlers from Russia to replace the Muslims he had driven out. He was happy to move whole populations about like pawns.

In 1565, Ivan went further, deciding to divide his kingdom into two: the *Oprichnina*, the area round Moscow, which was

Opposite: Ivan killed his heir-apparent Ivan Ivanovich in a fit of violent rage: here he holds the dying youth by his bloodied head.

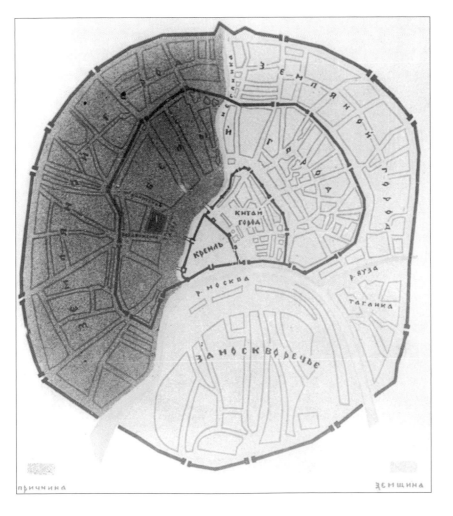

Left: Moscow's administrative zones, as ordained by Ivan the Terrible, who pursued a policy of 'divide-and-rule' from his court to the country as a whole.

BEWARE OF THE DOG-HEAD

MOUNTED ON BLACK HORSES and garbed in coarse black gowns that gave them a macabre monkish air, the *Oprichniki* were a dreadful sight. They cut off the heads of dogs and hung them from their horses' bridles to show how ferociously they sniffed out sedition and snapped at the insubordinate, and had brushes on their riding crops to show how they swept the country clear of traitors.

They were a tough, unfeeling crew, carefully selected from the lowest ranks of the gentry, or even the peasantry: their overwhelming loyalty was to the Czar himself. Ivan's strategy was about centring power upon himself at the expense of the traditional elite – those noble dynasties he couldn't help fearing as a threat.

The *Oprichniki*'s brutality was not just notorious; it was their badge of honour. The more capricious and cruel they were, the better their commander liked it. They were not just a praetorian guard for the Czar; they were openly his instrument of terror.

Opposite: Boris Godunov has both regal and religious authority in this portrait by Ilya Glazunov (1930–2017). Even so, it seems, he can't protect his people.

to be held under his own direct control, and the *Zemshchina*, which was to be run by a boyars' council. However, Ivan's 6000-strong secret police force, the black-cowled *Oprichniki*, while (as their name suggests) living around their ruler in the *Oprichnina*, were allowed (indeed encouraged) to roam the *Zemshchina* at will. They terrorized the population there, pulling in suspects for torture sessions in which Ivan himself apparently took an eager part.

The population of the *Zemshchina* was swollen by the stream of noble families ejected from the *Oprichnina* and forced to leave ancestral lands to find new homes elsewhere. In 1566, more than 12,000 men, women and children were forced from their lands by the *Oprichniki* and sent trudging off on foot with such belongings as they could carry through the winter snow. Any peasant who tried to help them – even by burying the bodies of the many who collapsed and died – was seized and executed on the spot.

The clerical-looking cowls of the *Oprichniki* perhaps signal that same sense of dressing up and carnival that we saw in Ivan's show trials. The attackers at least seem to have enjoyed their sprees of rape. In some villages, women and girls were made to strip naked and chase chickens about their fields and catch them. Anything for fun.

THEY STARTED BEING DENOUNCED AS 'ENEMIES OF THE PEOPLE', THEIR BODIES HANGED OUTSIDE THE FRONTS OF PUBLIC BUILDINGS.

SUSPICION COMES FULL CIRCLE

Setting one part of his country against the other may have helped shore up the Czar's authority, but it made it an authority over a much weaker state. This officially sanctioned civil war was literally self-destructive. In 1571, Ivan was helpless in the face of an invading Tatar army that even ransacked part of his capital. And his Russia retreated into itself: his hopes of annexing Livonia and so of more or less controlling the Baltic region had ultimately to be abandoned as unrealistic.

It was only a matter of time before the Czar who had formed the *Oprichniki* started to see them as being as much of a threat as the aristocracy he had created them to crush. And rightly so: their leaders had grown immensely powerful. From around 1572 onward, they started being denounced as 'enemies of the people', their bodies hanged outside the fronts of public buildings. Again came the bleakly comic, carnivalesque note: Prince Andrei Ovtsyn (whose surname resembles the Russian word for 'sheep') was hanged beside a bleating ewe outside the *Oprichniki* headquarters. Another leading *Oprichnik* who had aspired to see the Czar marry his sister had to watch her being raped by 500 common soldiers.

Убїенїе Стаго влаговѣрнаго Цревича Кнзѧ Димитрїа московскагѡ и всеѧ Рѡссїи, новагѡ
Чꙋдотворца.

When he died in 1584, Ivan left behind a drained, exhausted Russia, and a drained, exhausted Czar in his son Feodor I (1557–98). He let his brother-in-law Boris Godunov (*c*.1551–1605) rule on his behalf; he reigned on as Czar in his own right for seven years after Feodor died.

FAMINE AND FIGHTING

By comparison with Ivan the Terrible, just about any head of state would have seemed benign and judicious. Godunov, however, really did try to be those things. But his reign was stalked by disaster too, starting in 1601 with what was arguably the country's worst ever famine, in which an estimated two million people – a third of the population – died.

The political situation became volatile. Godunov was toppled in that bewildering montage of violence and tumult known to historians as the 'Time of Troubles'; his place was taken by a new Czar, Dmitri I, or the 'False Dmitri'. Dmitri claimed to be the youngest son of Ivan the Terrible (the real prince is believed to have died long before). 'Dmitri' had, he insisted, been hidden away by his mother Maria Nagaya for his own safety. Now he had come back to lead Russia. It hardly mattered who he was, given the anarchic state the nation was in, its difficulties compounded by an invasion by the Polish-Lithuanian Commonwealth. In 1606, Dmitri was chased from his palace and murdered by a mob of boyars, making way for Czar Vasili IV (1552–1612).

A further period of Polish domination brought Vladislav IV (1595–1648) to the throne in both countries, but while he remained in power in Poland he was ousted in Russia, where Czar Michael I (1596–1645) was crowned in 1613. Michael's reign was unremarkable, but its aftermath was to be historic. The first Czar of the Romanov line, Michael was at the head of a succession that endured all the way through to the Revolution of 1917.

Above: Michael I looks as nondescript here as a reigning monarch reasonably could: his great importance was as inaugurator of the Romanov dynasty.

Opposite: The original Czarevich Dmitri had, some claimed, been murdered in childhood, as dramatically recorded here; others insisted he'd escaped.

3

'I WRITE ON HUMAN SKIN...'

Even modernizing rulers in Russia relied on autocracy and absolutism, their subjects the passive medium in which they worked.

I N 1773, the French *philosophe* Denis Diderot (1713–84) paid a visit to St Petersburg at the invitation of Russia's ruler, Catherine the Great (1729–96). He came fresh from completing one of the great creative monuments of the European 'Enlightenment': the 28-volume *Encyclopédie* (1751–72). The *Encyclopédistes* – the group of writers who had produced this work – had been at odds with the *Ancien Regime* in their own country. Between the Church, with its spirituality of superstition, and the monarchic state, reactionary and repressive, it had meant a denial of freedom and all possibility of progress. '*Écrasez l'infâme*' – 'obliterate the infamy' – François-Marie Arouet (1694–1778) had written. However, Voltaire, as he is better known, had kept a portrait of the Russian empress in his bedroom. They had never met, but had corresponded for years. Catherine had supported him with her friendship, just as she had supported Diderot and his *Encyclopédie* with her funds.

Opposite: An enlightened tyrant, a humanitarian despot, a courageous reformer and a fierce reactionary, Catherine the Great embodied key contradictions of Russian history.

Diderot had come to thank Catherine for this life- and Enlightenment-saving support. He was intrigued by the thought of meeting her as well – justifiably, it turned out. Hers was a lively, avidly curious intellect, and she had thought much about her responsibilities as a ruler. 'You *philosophes* are fortunate,' she told her French visitor. 'You write on unfeeling paper. I write on human skin, which is sensitive to the slightest touch.'

THE HUMAN FACTOR

Just a few years previously, Catherine II had recommended a more robust way of writing on human skin. She had prescribed the 'knout' (a multi-stranded scourge) for any peasant who complained against his landlord. Hypocrisy is hardly unusual, but was there a deeper, more toxic, pathology at play here? Catherine's view of herself as an author on the one hand acknowledges the human impact of her rule, but at the same time dehumanizes her subjects almost completely.

Radical reform has always come with risks. The betterment of the masses brings with it a threat to the welfare and happiness of the individual. The political fulfilment of Voltaire and Diderot's intellectual project, the French Revolution of 1789, was to be closely followed by the Reign of Terror. Russian history, however, has often carried this contradiction to extremes: idealism and fanaticism, aspiration and atrocity, have gone hand in hand.

Born in 1672, Peter I became 'Second Czar' at the age of 11; his elder half-brother Ivan V (1666–96) was mentally handicapped.

Below: Whilst Diderot's meeting with Catherine II suggests a darker side to the Enlightenment, it also emblematizes Russia's tendency to impose improvements 'from the top down'.

Although he had not suffered the abuse that Ivan IV had, Russia's royal household had been no place for a child. Not long before his accession, Peter had seen his mentor and father figure Artamon Matveyev (1625–82), the late Czar's friend and counsellor, hacked to death before his eyes. Up to 40 other relatives had been cruelly killed.

The *Streltsy*, elite soldiers who carried firearms, had risen up in response to the death of Peter's older brother, Fyodor III (1661–82), fearing that the influence that they had built up during his reign would be lost. Matveyev's killing cleared the way for Peter's half-sister, Sophia Alekseyevna (1657–1704), to hold real power, with the *Streltsy*'s backing. Peter only succeeded in wresting power from her in 1689 so he could reign in his own right. Ivan's death in 1696 ratified Peter's position as Russia's ruler: his ambitions for his country were apparent from the start.

Above: The *Streltsy* were a force to be reckoned with, not only on the battlefield but in the political arena in the Russia of the seventeenth-century.

Above: Peter I's tour of
Western Europe took
him not just to courts
and art collections but to
industrial sites like this
shipyard in Deptford,
southeast London.

WAR AND WESTERNIZATION

In 1696, Peter won his first victory in war, taking the Black
Sea port of Azov from the Turks. This served notice of Russia's
emergence as a military power, and identified Russia with the
cause of the Christian West. Till now, trade between Russia and
Western Europe had been compelled to pass through the port of
Archangelsk on the White Sea, far to the north, and ice-bound
half the year.

His warm-water port secured, Peter set out on his 'Grand
Embassy': an extended tour of the Western countries. Travelling
incognito, he observed everything from etiquette to the arts.
He took in public lectures, visited factories and shipyards, and
even received training as a carpenter. Back in Russia, he tried to
inculcate the ideas and attitudes he had encountered in the West.
He began with a symbolic gesture, ordering his boyars to shave
off their beards (he actually introduced a tax on lengthy beards),
and encouraging the introduction of French fashion and language
in high society.

Peter brought in foreign craftsmen and scientists and promoted education on an unprecedented scale. He built a modern Western-style navy and reformed Russian institutions such as the army and civil service. He placed himself in charge of the Church's land and buildings, boosting both his tax revenues and his power in the land. Those 'Old Believers' who had refused to accept the ecclesiastical reforms of the earlier 17th century were penalized with a separate tax.

BALTIC OVERTURES

Peter's admiration for all things Western did not prevent him from picking quarrels with his European neighbours, notably

TERROR OF THE *TEREM*

AN UPPER-CLASS WOMAN'S place in 17th-century Russia was not just in the home but in the *terem*: a secluded section of the house, generally upstairs, away from strangers. This makes Sophia Alekseyevna's assertion of authority as her younger brothers' regent, and the ruthlessness with which she carried out this role, the more remarkable. Alexis I (*c*.1625–69) had left behind two families by his successive wives. Alekseyevna used Ivan – and for some time Peter – as a means to her own ends.

Alekseyevna also used the *Streltsy* as a sort of private army for advancing her political ends. After Fyodor's death, she had proposed to the Orthodox Church that, rather than be passed over, her full-brother Ivan should reign under her own regency, and young Peter be just a 'Second Czar'. The prelates had initially refused, but she made a deal with the *Streltsy* to get her way.

Above: Sophia Alekseyevna was the first of several strong and ruthless female Russian rulers.

with Sweden, which was then the main power in the Baltic. The Great Northern War (1700–21) reflected Peter's resolve to register Russia's presence on the world stage. It also showed his determination to reorientate Russia geopolitically: access to the Baltic as well as to the Black Sea meant a more immediate 'window on the West'. By 1703, he was in a position to found a fort at the mouth of the River Neva, looking out across the Baltic; by 1712, he had built a new capital on the site, named (in his honour) St Petersburg.

HE TOOK A PERSONAL PART IN THE PUNISHMENT OF THOSE WHO HAD BEEN CAPTURED, 1200 OF WHOM WERE TORTURED AND KILLED.

Russia had continued to take shape with Moscow as its centre, a city far from coasts or borders – landlocked, both literally and in its cast of mind. In creating this new Baltic metropolis, Peter was tilting Russia on its traditional axis. (It was with Peter's reign that it became customary for Russia's Czar to be referred to as its

Left: His air appropriately visionary, Peter stands on the site which will one day be his capital – and, of course, for most of its history, bear his name.

'Emperor' – the country's expanding territories justified the title.)

Built on what had been empty saltmarsh, St Petersburg was conceived along the most modern Western lines, with wide boulevards and sweeping terraces of stone-built houses. The views it offered over the Neva River were dramatic, its spectacular skylines picked out with palaces and churches. It boasted street-lighting, paved sidewalks and public parks. Crucially, St Petersburg was also a seaport: not only did it open a window to overseas trade and cultural commerce, but also announced Russia's arrival as a naval power.

TOUGH LOVE

Peter's reformist glove concealed an iron hand, as made clear when, shortly after his return from his Grand Embassy in 1698, Moscow's *Streltsy* attempted to rise up a second time. Not only did the Czar have the rebels put down without mercy, he took a personal part in the punishment of those who had been captured, 1200 of whom were tortured and killed, their bodies publicly displayed.

Opposite: His victory at Poltava (6 June 1709) was a turning-point for Peter, giving him the upper hand in the Great Northern War.

BUILT ON BONES

ONE OF THE WORLD'S most stunning cities had been raised up on the mass graves of tens of thousands of Russian serfs and Swedish prisoners-of-war who had been worked to death in its construction. Over half a million peasants laboured there, their efforts donated by their landowners in response to the Czar's decree that every owner of 500 or more serfs had to contribute a two-storey building in the city. Russia's serfs were not soft; backbreaking labour was their lot in life. However, living in dirty, disease-ridden swamps for months on end, with only improvised shanties for shelter and meagre sustenance, up to a fifth of those who came to work there never left. They were buried where they fell, in the foundations of the new city. In this too, however, St Petersburg was a fitting symbol for a czar who pursued his modernizing goals without regard to human cost.

Peter was also domineering with the women in his life. He sent his first wife, Eudoxia Lopukhina (1669–1731), to a convent when he tired of her. He had previously learned that she had taken a young officer as a lover, and had that unfortunate individual cut into quarters, so she must have felt lucky to escape the marriage in one piece. His long-term mistress, the Dutch-born Anna Mons (1672–1714), was also sidelined, sent into internal exile when she fell in love with another man. Peter eventually allowed the lovers to marry.

In 1707, Peter himself married Martha Skavronskaya (1684–1727), a Polish peasant girl and later domestic servant, and made her his Czarina. The secret of her success as imperial spouse seems to have been her never-failing cheerfulness in the face of all his rages. Peter even seems to have forgiven her rumoured affair with Anna Mons' brother Willem (1688–1724), although legend has it that Willem wasn't so lucky. He was executed and his head embalmed and sent to Martha so she could contemplate it and learn her lesson. Even so, she reigned after Peter's death as Empress Catherine I.

FLOGGING IN THE FAMILY

Peter's eldest son, Alexei (1690–1718), had been caught in the bitterness that had grown up between his mother, Eudoxia Lopukhina, and his father. The boyars who brought him up were antagonistic towards the Czar as well. Alexei grew up bookish and spiritual, too – quite unlike his father. Relations between them were always uneasy when, in 1716, Peter sent Alexei to oversee a shipbuilding project in the provinces. Instead, Alexei fled to Vienna, refusing to return.

After almost a year's absence, he was tempted back by Peter's promise that he would be safe and allowed to go unpunished. Instead, he was arrested, members of his entourage tortured, their feet burned or their flesh picked at with red-hot pincers before being impaled or broken on a wheel. In their agonies,

Below: The execution of the *Streltsy*, 1699, both secured and underscored Czar Peter's power. Violence has always been an adjunct of authority in Russian history.

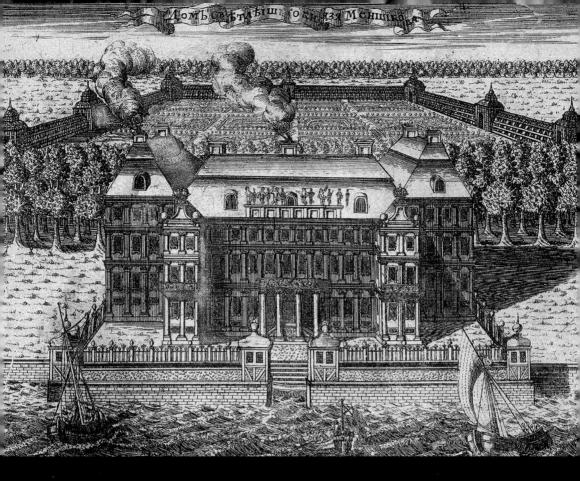

Above: St Petersburg's governor-general, Prince Alexander Menshikov (1673–1729), built this palace from the spoils of his corrupt reign.

some uttered incriminating accusations against Alexei, so he was arrested and tortured in his turn. On the basis of no real evidence, he was convicted of plotting against his father's life and condemned to 40 lashes of the knout. The first 25 prostrated him, and he was allowed a day's respite. He was formally condemned to death, but in the event beat the executioner to it, fading away and dying within a few days of his flogging.

MODERNIZING MONSTER

Peter had followed some form of legal process, but he had killed his son as surely as Ivan the Terrible had Ivan Ivanovich, and coldly and deliberately rather than in a fit of rage. Peter was a frightening figure all round, with an intimidating, even thuggish, presence, standing almost 2.1m (7ft) tall and loud and aggressive in his manner.

Despite his pursuit of cultural and scientific knowledge, Peter had never been interested in these things for their own sake, only for their potential benefits for Russian prosperity and power. If his reforms made the armed forces and bureaucracy more meritocratic (and the aristocracy hungrier and less complacent), it was done simply to strengthen Russia – and himself. A law of 1721 helped jump-start Russian industry by allowing entrepreneurs to buy serfs

A MONUMENT TO CORRUPTION

ST PETERSBURG'S MENSHIKOV PALACE was built in 1710 for the city's first governor-general, Prince Alexander Menshikov (1673–1729). Peter's affection for this friend proved extraordinarily enduring, for Menshikov's avarice was evident from the first. Leading military expeditions in Poland, he had come back laden with booty – not from the battlefield, but from the accounts of his own army.

The building of the palace was one of the world's biggest building projects in its time; for Menshikov, it was also one of the world's greatest opportunities for taking bribes. There was so much work to be done, so many major projects to be undertaken, so many contracts to be issued, so many purchases and requisitions to be made…it would have been a temptation for the most scrupulous, and Menshikov was a crook. Fabulously rich already by the time his benefactor died, he then made himself the power behind Catherine I's throne – and in so doing made himself another fortune.

Above: Prince Menshikov made a fortune in bribery and embezzlement as St Petersburg's governor.

In the end, though, his enemies among the old aristocracy got the better of him. Menshikov was brought down, stripped of his rank and riches and exiled to Siberia.

like slaves from rural landowners. This advanced the economy but showed contempt for the notion of 'human rights'.

THE ACCIDENTAL EMPRESS

Peter died in 1725, and a succession of women rulers followed, although Martha's succession to her late husband's throne as the Empress Catherine I owed more to intriguing at court than cunning on her part. Elements of the 'Old Nobility' marginalized by Peter were anxious to return to a place of power, and 'New Men' – most notably Menshikov – were as anxious to prevent them.

IF SHE WAS STUCK AT HOME, SHE ENJOYED TAKING POT SHOTS AT PASSING ANIMALS FROM HER PALACE WINDOWS.

In the event, the New Men won: Menshikov was effectively Russia's ruler, even awarding himself the ceremonial title *Generalissimus*. In the confusion following Catherine's death in 1727, however, the Old Nobility managed to organize against Menshikov before he could cement his place by putting his daughter on the throne as the new Czar's bride. Peter II (1715–30) died as soon as Menshikov could have wished, aged only 14, but his title passed to Anna Ivanovna, daughter of Peter the Great's elder brother, Ivan V, in 1730.

HUNTING AND HURTING

Although not quite the puppet Catherine I had been, Anna had little apparent interest in ruling Russia. She had married young, to a German nobleman. He had died within a few weeks of their wedding, and she had spent the years since ruling his duchy as its regent. As Czarina, it was widely said that her heart still lay in Germany; she herself took solace in the German arms of Ernst Johann von Biron (1690–1772), her counsellor and lover.

Opposite: She may seem to have the whip hand in this portrait (*c*.1729) but Catherine I was pretty much a puppet of powerful factions at her own court.

Broadly speaking, Anna is regarded as having continued the programme of Westernization that Peter the Great had started, but she more or less shunned the boring business of government. Lively and light-hearted, albeit with a vicious streak, she loved hunting. If she was stuck at home, she enjoyed taking pot shots at passing animals from her palace windows.

Anna had an almost equal passion for playing practical jokes upon her courtiers – sometimes sadistic ones. She was angry when Prince Mikhail Golitsyn (1687–75) converted to Catholicism to marry an Italian woman. Rather than taking pity when his bride died only a short time later, Anna triumphed, and gave the prince a position as her court jester. He had to pretend to be a chicken and lay eggs whenever a visitor came to court. She then forced him to marry her oldest maidservant. The couple were dressed in jesters' motley and paraded in public on an elephant's back, with a retinue of physically handicapped attendants, before being wed at an elaborate ceremony conducted in a specially constructed ice palace.

FROM BABY TO BEAUTY

Ivan VI (1740–64) succeeded Anna. Nominally at least, he interrupted the 'Petticoat' succession, but was only a couple of

Below: Jesters entertain the Empress Anna in her court. She shocked observers with her unsophisticated – and sometimes downright cruel – sense of fun.

months old when he became
Czar and only just turned one
when he was ousted. He cannot
have had any real idea of his
historical significance (although
he lived on, a prisoner, into his
twenties), and Russian history
scarcely registered his reign.
His mother, Anna Leopoldovna
(1718–46), had been his regent,
and their usurper was another
woman: Elizabeth (1709–62)
seized power in a coup in 1741.

A daughter of Peter the
Great and Martha/Catherine
I, Elizabeth felt she had been
cheated of her rightful throne.
Attractive and ultra-feminine in
her self-presentation, she was
the stereotypical steely beauty.
She turned up at a barracks of the imperial guard, wearing
armour round her upper body over her dress, demanding that the
officers and men come with her to help her claim her crown. Less
dramatic, but more important, she had also for some time been
gathering support from Russia's Old Nobility and France.

Above: Elizabeth makes
a melodramatic entrance
at the head of a column
of soldiers to seize power
from young Ivan VI
and his regent, Anna
Leopoldovna.

'THE RUSSIAN LADY IN FRENCH HEELS'

Elizabeth made a strong and confident empress. Her hyper-
feminine manner masked an accomplished political operator
and a capable administrator. Although she could be warm and
friendly, she was capricious, quick alike to swing in mood and
take offence. She was smart but no bluestocking. A fashion
fanatic, she changed her outfit several times a day, and never wore
the same dress twice. After her death, 15,000 of her gowns and
several thousand pairs of shoes were found in one residence alone.

Elizabeth's extravagant tastes began a sort of arms race at the
court: all the ladies felt they had to take their cue from her, and

TENDER MERCY

UNUSUALLY, not just for 18th-century Russia but for her age in general, Elizabeth made a resolution never to put anyone to death. She was hardly gentle, though, as Natalia Lopukhina (1699–1763) and her friend Anna Bestuzheva (dates unknown) were to find in 1743. Lopukhina and Elizabeth already had history: Natalia had been acclaimed as the 'brightest flower' of Anna's court, to Elizabeth's chagrin, and it was no secret that Elizabeth did not rate too high in Lopukhina's estimation.

Elizabeth came to suspect that Lopukhina and Bestuzheva were involved in a conspiracy to topple her. There seems to be little evidence for this, but, with Western countries such as France concerned to rein in Russia's power, and German states such as Holstein interested by virtue of the late Empress Anna's marriage, there was scope for speculation and suspicion.

Natalia and Anna were arraigned and tried, found guilty, then stripped naked before being paraded through the city. They were flogged about the buttocks with knouts, and were then to have their tongues torn out. Bestuzheva had bribed the executioner to put only a nick in her tongue. Natalia took another tack, biting his hand as he reached into her mouth, with

Above: Floggings in eighteenth-century Russia were not just a form of punishment but a public spectacle.

the result that he yanked her whole tongue out by the roots.

As the two women stood weeping and bleeding, their male 'co-conspirators' (the British ambassador's view that there was nothing to the conspiracy more than a little insubordinate gossip) were broken on the wheel. This meant they were stretched out starfish-like across cartwheels placed on the ground, their hands and feet tied down, while men with sledgehammers smashed the bones of all their limbs in multiple places. Finally, for good measure, they were all exiled to Siberia to end their days.

try to match her change for change. But woe betide the woman who upstaged the empress or accidentally wore an outfit – even an accessory – that looked too much like hers. Only Elizabeth could wear pink. Some unfortunate ladies found the angry empress taking a pair of scissors to over-luxuriant locks; one woman who accidentally wore the same gown as her was struck hard across the face. Once, when an ambitious hair treatment went wrong and the empress was forced to shave her head completely, every other lady at court was forced to do the same.

Elizabeth knew that marriage would mean surrendering personal power and risk rocking the precarious equilibrium between Russia's noblest families. Her long-term lover, Alexei Razumovsky (1709–71), knew his place, which was very much in the background, although his emotional support seems to have been important to the empress. As she was childless, though, she had to find an heir.

After Elizabeth's death in 1762, the throne passed to Peter III (1728–62). He was Holstein born and bred, the grandson of Peter the Great and Martha/Catherine I. He never took to Russia; nor did Russia take to him. After six months' Czardom, he was ousted by his own Czarina (and second cousin), Sophia Augusta Frederica, better known to history as Catherine II, or Catherine the Great.

Below: French portraitist Louis Caravaque (1684–1754) captured the elegance and poise of the Empress Elizabeth – along with her immense hauteur.

PORTRAIT OF A MARRIAGE

Peter and Catherine had married in 1745, but their match had been nakedly dynastic from the start. Even by those standards, though, it had been unhappy. Weakly built and badly pockmarked, Peter was also immature, continuing with the games of soldiers he had loved (and that Catherine found contemptible) when she had first met him at the age of 11. His whole life, she would afterwards recall, had been a 'constant childhood'. Bullied into the marriage in the first place by her own overbearing mother, and bullied into compliance thereafter as her complaints accumulated and unhappiness accrued, she was bullied by the Empress Elizabeth as well.

As for Catherine's relations with her husband, they were 'monstrous, degrading', one commentator wrote:

He made her the confidante of his amorous intrigues. Drunk from the age of ten, he came one night in liquor to entertain his wife with a description of the graces and charms of the daughter of Biron; and as Catherine pretended to be asleep, he gave her a punch with his fist to awaken her. This booby kept a kennel of dogs, which infested the air, at the side of his wife's bedchamber, and hung rats in his own, to punish them according to the rules of martial law.

THE GERMAN CONNECTION

Ernst Johann von Biron, now getting on in years, had been the lover and life companion to the Empress Anna, but he still had a presence and some power around the court. He represented another link with Germany for a Czar who had never relinquished that connection. As if his war games weren't silly enough, the fact that Peter had brought in a company of guardsmen from Holstein (and that he dressed as Frederick the

Opposite: He's no oil-painting, perhaps, but Peter III is nevertheless captured here in all his effeteness. Portraitist Aleksey Antropov (1716–95) was the consummate professional.

Below: It's the defiance of its stance that makes Catherine II's St Petersburg statue so convincing – that, and the clustering of men beneath her feet.

Great to marshal them) made what might have been merely irritating actually offensive for the Russians.

Catherine too was German, but she identified with her adopted homeland, partly out of loathing for her husband, but also from the ambition her humiliations and frustrations only fed. Catherine shared the fears of the St Petersburg elite that Peter's reign was taking Russia too close diplomatically to Germany – particularly to the Prussia of Frederick the Great (1712–86). She had also become convinced (not without reason) that she would make a much more effective ruler than her husband.

GRIGORY ORLOV, WE KNOW, HAD BEEN NOT JUST A LOVER BUT AN IMPORTANT MEANS TO THE END OF IMPERIAL POWER.

CATHERINE'S COUP

Catherine made her move in July 1762, while Peter was away at his seaside summer palace in Oranienbaum, beside the Gulf of Finland. Catherine had him arrested and forced him to sign

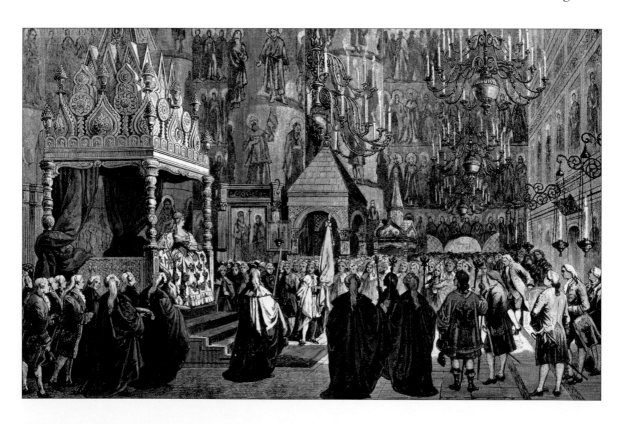

a letter of abdication. Alexei Orlov (1737–1807) seems to have taken it upon himself to have Peter murdered in prison, but Catherine was happy enough to shower him with grants and positions of influence thereafter. Alexei's brother, Grigory (1734–83), was Catherine's lover and co-conspirator: the family did very well out of her accession.

SEX AND THE MODERN MONARCH

Catherine took many lovers. 'My heart', she confided in a letter to the most famous of them, Grigory Alexandrovich Potemkin (1739–91), 'is reluctant to remain even an hour without love.' What she means by 'love' in this sentence isn't clear. Is it just a euphemistic way of saying 'sex', as some have concluded? Or was this 'man-eater' actually admitting to a real, and ultimately emotional, vulnerability?

Above: This portrait of Prince Potemkin offers us a picture within a picture: he has a miniature of his lover Catherine pinned to his chest.

Historian Simon Sebag-Montefiore has pointed out that what amounted to an ongoing *ménage à trois* – albeit one whose third party frequently changed – gave Catherine a quasi – 'family'. There is no doubt, though, that between her personality and her position in life, the empress not only had far more freedom of action than most women of her time but a much greater readiness to acknowledge and act upon her desires.

That her desires might be fulfilled within her marriage was evidently ridiculous. She took up with her attendant Sergei Saltykov (1726–65) shortly after her arrival in Russia. A few years later, she had a passionate affair with the future king of Poland, Stanislav Poniatowski (1732–98), while he was staying in St Petersburg (1755–6). Grigory Orlov, we know, had been not just a lover but an important means to the end of imperial power. She remained grateful to him for his help but soon moved on. By 1772, she was in a liaison with Ensign Alexander Vasilchikov (1744–1813).

Opposite: The great ceremony and splendour surrounding Catherine's coronation in September 1762 helped obscure the deep irregularity of her accession.

VILLAGES AND CITIES

FOR FILM BUFFS, THE name 'Potemkin' will be
associated with the famous 'Battleship' of
Sergei Eisenstein's great movie of 1925 and
the historical episode on which it was based.
The man himself is popularly associated
with the idea of the 'Potemkin Village'. A
mock-up, picturesquely painted, but all
façade; these 'communities' supposedly
sprang up wherever the empress went,
to reassure her of the contentment and
prosperity of her subjects. Once the imperial
coach had passed, they could be dismantled
and moved to be set up anew a little further
on in her journey.

Irresistible as the story is, there is no
evidence that such villages existed. Potemkin
did, however, as *Namestnik* (Viceroy) of
Catherine's newly conquered territories in
Crimea and along the Black Sea coast, build
new cities such as Odessa and Sevastopol.

Above: The 'Potemkin Village': happy peasants greet
their queen whilst more dourly-dressed villagers lurk
out of sight.

At some point in the early 1770s, Catherine embarked
on her relationship with Potemkin. A dashing general,
diplomat and statesman, he does in hindsight look much more
interesting than the general run of the empress's favourites. Her
relationship with him was deeper, and may have extended as far
as secret marriage. Neither was willing to surrender their sexual
independence, though. Both took lovers, but remained with one
another in between.

This may sound like a highly modern and sophisticated
polyamorous relationship, but it was not short of old-fashioned
jealousies and tensions. Even so, it functioned over many years

in its own fashion. From 1776, Catherine was sleeping with her secretary, Pyotr Zavadovsky (1739–1812). He was followed by Semyon Zorich (1744–99), a Serbian count and lieutenant general in the Imperial Russian Army; Ivan Rimsky-Korsakov (1754–1831); Alexander Lanskoy (1758–84); Alexander Yermolov (1754–1834), and Alexander Dmitriev-Mamonov (1758–1803). As Catherine became older, her lovers (Potemkin excepted) did not. Prince Platon Zubov (1767–1822), with whom the empress had an affair between 1789 and 1796, had still been some years away from being born when (already 33) she had ascended his country's throne.

PUGACHEV AND PETER

There is little evidence to suggest that Czar Peter III was seriously missed, but the injustices he had suffered became a rallying point for opposition. Agrarian unrest was an inseparable part of life as an agrarian economy in the 18th century – the more so when, as in Russia, medieval conditions still prevailed. In so far

Below: 'Czar Peter' Pugachev administers opera buffa village justice in this painting by Vasily Perov (1834–82).

as she was a modernizer, Catherine was concerned to strengthen the hand of innovative landowners, at the expense of what the rural poor saw as age-old rights and privileges. The net effect of 'progress' seemed to be that they were much worse off. The old 'feudal' system might have tied them to the land, but the new one threatened to make them much more like the master's property – the 'serfs' were in danger of becoming slaves.

If the peasantry were permanently unhappy, they were by no means the only ones. The Old Believers were entrenched in their anger. Successive empresses had only strengthened those discriminatory measures introduced by Peter the Great

A 'MYSTIC OFFICE'

The position of First Maid of Honour was an extraordinarily important one, given the access and attention it could command, especially with a woman on the throne. Catherine could confide in Maria Perekusikhina (1739–1824) through the 1760s and, in later years, in Anna Protasova (1745–1826), in a way she couldn't with her male courtiers.

The English poet Lord Byron (1788–1824) came over coy when, in *Don Juan,* he referenced 'Miss Protasoff', her informal title and her supposed duties, prepared to say no more than that she was

'Named from her mystic office "l'Épreuveuse",

A term inexplicable to the Muse...'

The French word means 'trialler' or 'tester'; sources vary on what she was testing *for.* Legend has it that she was 'road testing' Catherine's choice of lovers for virility, checking that they would be sufficiently

Above: Anna Protasova was Catherine's close confidante in her later years.

good in bed. More cautious scholars have suggested a less raunchy (though equally unromantic) purpose: that of screening prospective partners for syphilis.

to discourage adherence to what was seen as a backward-looking and potentially disruptive movement. The Cossacks of Russia's southern and eastern territories shared the discontents of both groups: many were actually Old Believers, and all were affected by Catherine's landholding reforms.

HE DIDN'T CALL THE PEOPLE TO ARMS IN ANGER AND IDEALISM, BUT IMPOSED A DRAFT – ONE RECRUIT FROM EVERY SECOND FAMILY.

Into the midst of what was already a highly volatile situation stepped Yemelyan Pugachev (*c.*1742–75), a madman-visionary of the sort so often at the centre of popular revolts over the ages. Russia itself, we have seen, had witnessed second, third and fourth comings of Ivan the Terrible's son Dmitri. Pugachev, although his background in the Volga was well documented, claimed to be the Emperor Peter III who, far from dying in 1762, had actually escaped.

A CARNIVAL OF KILLING

Not for the first time in Russian history, life imitated carnival: Pugachev did not so much stage a rising as set up an alternate state. Like Catherine's Empire in dress-up, it had its own bureaucracy, which produced official-sounding statements and letters (written by local priests), and its own civil servants and nobles. Pugachev, of course, was Czar Peter, but below him there was an array of important-sounding officials and aristocratically titled nobles. He didn't call the people to arms in anger and idealism, but imposed a draft – one recruit from every second family. They were not rising in rebellion but serving their state and their Czar.

In September 1773, Pugachev's forces took the town of Samara, before going on to occupy the city of Kazan, where the Volga and Kazanka rivers meet. By the middle of 1774, the rebels held a major swathe of the region to the west of the Urals, but their alternative Empire was living on borrowed time. Caught napping by the uprising's outbreak, but by now beginning to get organized, Catherine's army started making inroads on the rebels' 'Russia'.

Above: Pugachev's rising is seen starkly in class-war terms in 'The Assault of Kazan' by Otto Friedrich von Möller (1812–74).

Opposite: The Imam Sheikh Mansur became both a religious and a patriotic leader to the Chechens, for whom he remains a hero to this day.

At Tsaritsyn (now Volgograd), a vindictive Imperial Army killed 10,000 of Pugachev's followers. He himself escaped the field, but his spell was broken and he was betrayed, sold out by some who had formerly been his most loyal comrades. He was taken to Moscow and executed – beheaded and dismembered before a crowd in Bolotnaya Square – on 21 January 1775.

THE CHECHEN CONFLICT

Gradually expanding under Catherine, the Russian Empire was beginning to establish a presence in the northern Caucasus, largely by a series of supposed police actions, designed to prevent raids on its own southern frontiers.

The Caucasus was a patchwork of peoples, fiercely patriotic and well armed: resistance to the Russians was the one thing they had in common. The pseudo-scientific theories that would underpin Western imperialism in Africa and East Asia (and, ultimately, Nazism in Germany) were still some way off, but the Russians still saw their 'European' status as setting them apart from (and above) the 'natives' in these 'uncivilized' places.

In 1783, the men of the Nogay people had chosen to kill their own women and children before fighting to the death themselves in their tens of thousands rather than allow themselves to be conquered by the Russians. Anger at the brutality of these Russian actions, reaching a simmering point in Chechnya, boiled over in 1785. It found leadership in a local Muslim teacher, or *imam*, Sheikh Mansur (1760–94), who mobilized his people in a programme of national renewal. Till now, at least, many Chechens had been pagans; those who had been Muslims had been comparatively lukewarm in their beliefs. Sheikh Mansur made the freedom struggle a spiritual one as well, the fight against Russia a version of *jihad*. A force of 5000 soldiers sent into Chechnya to arrest him found him gone from his home village; the community was massacred and their homes

EROTIC INTERIOR

IN ANY OTHER CONTEXT, the story of Catherine's 'Erotic Cabinet' would seem too extravagantly fantastical to be true. However, absolute power brings all but absolute ability to see one's fantasies realized. Hence, this notorious creation – a 'cabinet' in the old-fashioned sense of 'room' or 'apartment' fitted out as a tribute to the joys of love. Pornographic paintings decked its walls from floor to ceiling. Elaborately carved wooden furniture featured copulating couples. They disported themselves in a variety of positions and every imaginable gender, age and even species combination. Tables, chairs and couches had scrotums or women's breasts by way of feet, ejaculating penises arching up to serve as legs, and exuberant vulval flourishes left, right and centre.

razed. This action set the tone for what was to be a decades-long (even centuries-long) struggle in which bloody reprisals followed opportunistic guerrilla raids.

LEGENDS AND LIES

In the years that followed Pugachev's uprising, no fewer than 13 further Peter IIIs appeared, even if none came close to toppling Catherine. That they gained any traction with the people showed how strong anger was in the Russian countryside. In these febrile times, many had found it easy to be pretend-Peters, so why wouldn't there be a pretend-Catherine as well? This one was not an individual interloper, but the reputation of the empress, which threatened to eclipse the real woman almost completely.

Catherine had made enemies in the cities and further up the social scale as well: no real reformer could have avoided this. Certainly, no reforming female ruler could have avoided this; hence the misogyny inherent in the myth that the empress had died during copulation with a horse. The frame supporting the stallion above her body had broken, the story went, so half a ton of charger had fallen on top of her and crushed her. Less unkind, though still undignified, was the suggestion that she had died while seated on the lavatory. She had had a stroke and died in situ, it was said. This had at least a touch of truth: Catherine had indeed been taken ill during a bathroom visit, though she had lived several days longer and died in her own bed in 1796.

'BEATING UP THE JEWS'

'You arrive at a small town. How are you going to amuse yourself? You can't always be beating up the Jews…'. Set in the time of Pugachev's Rebellion, although written some decades later by Alexander Pushkin (1799–1837), *The Captain's Daughter* might really have been set at any time. What shocks us in Pushkin's speaker is the blandness of his bigotry; the absence of obvious malevolence or hatred in what he has to say; his easy-going acceptance of racist violence as default.

One recurring feature of Russian history has been the unappealing aspect worn by 'modernization'; the ruthlessness

Left: As seen by Britain's Isaac Cruickshank (1764–1811), Catherine is confronted in her final moments by the atrocities she's committed during her reign.

of what is presented as 'reform'. One corollary of this was the existence (and unreflecting acceptance) of anti-semitism among the supposedly intelligent and forward-looking. Peter the 'Great' he may have been, but Peter the Tolerant he wasn't: 'I prefer to see Muslims and Pagans in our midst than Jews,' he had said. 'They are rogues and cheats. I set out to eliminate evil, not to multiply it.'

Peter's daughter Elizabeth's first pronouncement on coming to the throne had been on the exclusive primacy of Orthodox Christianity in the Russian Empire. The 'Order of Expulsion' she announced allowed for any Jew who refused to convert to face banishment.

In the event, Russian society didn't have the organizational capacity to deliver on that threat, but Catherine the Great was the woman to get things done. In 1791, she established a 'Pale of Settlement' along the western margins of her empire. Extending from the Baltic to the Black Sea, it ran all the way down through Belarus and the Ukraine and took in the eastern edge of Prussia and western fringe of Russia. 90 per cent of Russia's Jews had to live here. And so, for the next century or more, they did, in *shtetls* – overwhelmingly Jewish settlements.

4

TIME AND PATIENCE

Napoleon notoriously underestimated the Russian people's capacity for soaking up affliction and then fighting back – but perhaps the Czars were to make the same mistake too.

I N HIS famous novel *War and Peace*, Russian writer Leo Tolstoy (1828–1910) maintains that 'The strongest of all warriors are these two – Time and Patience'. His was a fatalistic philosophy for which the truly heroic virtues were the passive ones of stoic endurance and acceptance of one's fate. The 'War' of his title was the invasion of his country by France's Emperor Napoleon I (1769–1821) in 1812 – one of the great military undertakings (and military disasters) of modern times. For Tolstoy, Napoleon's great mistake was to imagine that, as a man – a great man, even – he had the ability to shape not only his own fate but history.

Considered against the background of Russia's history as a whole, Tolstoy's theory doesn't totally convince. Russian leaders from Ivan the Terrible to Stalin have tried to bend their country's history to their will. The results may have been ghastly; they may not have shaped a history anyone in their right mind could possibly have wanted, but it can hardly be claimed that they

Opposite: Russian history has had a way of turning up destructive wild-cards, like the mesmerizing mystic, Grigori Rasputin.

Above: In the best
carnivalesque traditions
of Russian history, Count
Leo Tolstoy dressed as
a peasant to work
alongside the labourers
on his own estate.

completely failed. It is true, though, that, in 19th-century Russia, the most ambitious enterprises fell the flattest. The country was to be saved by that principle when the *Grande Armée* was sent packing in 1812; it was also to be brought crashing down by it in the Crimean War of 1853–5.

SPREAD THIN

When, on 24 June 1812, Napoleon crossed the River Nemen into Lithuania, it was at the head of the greatest invasion force so far seen. It was overkill, really, intended to make a surgical strike of a strategic sideshow: Russia's support of Britain and her allies had been an irritant to Imperial France, no more.

Before a shot had been fired, however, Napoleon's army was suffering serious attrition, losing 10,000 men in the four days it took to reach Vilnius. More important, from a military perspective, they had lost a similar number of horses. The lack of roads and an already overstretched supply line were posing problems. In the heat and rain of the Baltic summer, the going was swampy and the atmosphere unhealthy; many thousands of men were taken sick with flu.

If in hindsight it seems an act of hubris, Napoleon's first fatal error in mounting his invasion was not to underestimate but to overestimate his enemy – at least in the sense of misreading the state of development of their country. His plan had been that, as elsewhere in Europe, his army would live off the land as it advanced, seizing food reserves and confiscating livestock. Here, however, vast areas of low-productivity land had been managed to maintain low population densities. 'An army marches on its stomach,' Napoleon himself had said: these scabby fields could not keep so many soldiers going.

They continued to advance, although by the time they reached Smolensk on 16 August they were long past the point at which Napoleon had assumed the Czar would sue for peace. Rationally, this might have been the obvious course for Alexander I (1777–1825) to take. Instead, the Russians sat back and took their punishment – and saved the French the trouble of laying waste their land by burning enormous acreages in a literal 'scorched earth' strategy. Still the French came on, albeit in mounting anxiety and exasperation as the resolution they sought kept slipping away.

A HOLLOW VICTORY

The climactic engagement the French had been looking for finally came at Borodino, west of Moscow, where on 7 September a quarter of a million men clashed and tens of thousands lost their

Below: The Battle of Borodino, here imagined by the German painter Peter von Hess (1792–1871), was fought on an extraordinarily epic scale.

lives. Napoleon won the day and, the natural order of things apparently re-established, advanced in triumph on Moscow to take charge.

More than 100,000 troops entered the outskirts of the city on 14 September. They found the place in flames, apparently on the orders of its own governor, Fyodor Rostopchin (1763–1826). 'It was', wrote Napoleon, 'the most grand, the most sublime, and the most terrific sight the world ever beheld!' For those in the midst of it, however, it wasn't quite so poetic. This was a veritable firestorm, in which random tiles and indeed whole roofs flew through the air, given wings by the updraft, against

Below: Napoleon and his advancing force could only stare in helpless wonder as the prize they'd 'won' went up in smoke before their eyes.

a thunderous background noise of explosions from shops, warehouses, distilleries and ammunition stores.

As the days went by and the city went on burning, the French had the leisure to reflect on the sight of their hard-won conquest literally going up in smoke. Philosophically, they took possession of such palaces and townhouses that survived and settled in to wait for the surrender. However, that crucial, culminating moment never came. The Czar and his court had withdrawn to the east – in ostrich-like denial of the new reality, it might have been thought.

> IF WINTER WAS INDEED TO ATTACK HIS RETREATING FORCES IN THE REAR, HIS OWN DECISIONS MADE THEIR SITUATION MUCH WORSE.

Their refusal to play by the rules created a new reality all on its own. They were letting 'time and patience' win, in Tolstoyan terms. Five weeks after their arrival in the city, with no sign of the expected surrender coming, the French were forced to give up on a bad job and head for home.

Napoleon's defeat has often been attributed to 'General Winter', the idea being that the rigours of the Russian weather destroyed the French. However, the war was long since lost by the time the autumn came and Napoleon gave the order to withdraw. If winter was indeed to attack his retreating forces in the rear, his own decisions made their situation much worse. Against his marshals' advice, he chose to return the same way he had come – across the same not only poor, but previously plundered, territory. The Russians followed the same script too, avoiding direct engagement but harrying stragglers and picking off isolated groups sent out to get supplies.

COLD CARNIVAL

Comparatively rested and well fed after their furlough in Moscow, Napoleon's troops had set off in high spirits, despite their invasion's failure. They were burdened with booty, from candlesticks and crystal to aristocratic carriages. As the days went by and fatigue and hunger gripped, these were abandoned along the road, an impediment to those coming behind.

Above: The Retreat from Moscow became a favourite subject for artists addressing the perverseness of fortune and the pathos of war: this painting was produced in 1847.

Ladies' silks and satins (and, especially, fine fox and sable furs), brought as trophies, were forced into service against the cold. The men looked, one survivor wrote, 'like ghosts dressed up for a masquerade'.

The worst of it was the cold: by the beginning of November, the Russian winter had begun. The French – who had expected to be comfortably ensconced in Moscow by now – were completely unprotected. 'The cold grew more and more intense,' one man recalled:

the horses in the bivouacs died of hunger and cold. Every day some were left where we had passed the night.

The roads were like glass. The horses fell down, and could not get up. Our worn-out soldiers no longer had strength to their arms. The barrels of their muskets were so cold that they stuck to their hands. It was 28 degrees below zero. But the guard gave up their sacks and muskets only with their lives.

In order to save our lives, we had to eat the horses that fell down on the ice. The soldiers opened the skin with their knives and took out the entrails, which they roasted on the coals – if they had time to make a fire – and, if not, they ate them raw. They devoured the horses before they died...

Dogs and cats were killed and eaten – and, perhaps inevitably, fallen soldiers. On secondment from the British Army, General Sir Robert Wilson (1777–1849) was with the retreating troops. On one occasion, he recalled a group of men by a fire, 'sitting and lying over the body of a comrade which they had roasted, and which they had begun to eat.' Maddened by cold and hunger, men were seen trying to bite chunks out of their own bodies. Many were walking barefoot by now – the icy temperatures anaesthetized their extremities so completely they didn't register the pain of the skin and flesh being stripped from the bones beneath.

The nightmare deepened as the days went by. They weren't just walking across a bare, blizzard-blasted landscape but into an alien moral universe. 'Anyone who allowed himself to be affected by the deplorable scenes of which he was a witness condemned himself to death,' Captain Charles François (1774–1853) recalled; 'but the one who closed his heart to every feeling of pity found strength to resist any hardship.' Of the 500,000 men who had mounted the invasion, only 30,000 made it home.

HALF-HEARTED REFORM

Czar Alexander's victory had been won by a sort of heroic passivity, which set the tone for the remainder of his reign. He had ascended the throne in 1801 as a moderate reformer, rationalizing a sprawling and

Below: English artist George Dawe (1781–1829) painted a whole gallery of (over 300) portraits of those who'd helped defeat Napoleon. Alexander I had pride of place.

disorganized civil service and attempting to ease the condition of the serfs. But he had quickly lost the will to reform when faced with opposition from vested interests in government, and cracked down in the countryside when he saw unrest was being stirred. Briefly, in his first flush of idealist ardour, he had relaxed state censorship, only to recoil in rage when criticized.

The latter years of Alexander's reign were characterized by a curmudgeonly conservatism. In the winter of 1825, while on a trip to southern Russia for the sake of his ailing wife, Alexander fell sick himself. Within a few weeks he had died of typhus; the Czarina followed him soon after, and Russia was left without its ruling couple. Inevitably, there was speculation: the Czar had seemed fine when he left St Petersburg; many suspected he was still alive, his state funeral an elaborate charade.

DECEMBRIST DOWNFALL

THE RESULT OF CZAR Alexander's reign was a pent-up desire for political and social change on a scale that no modest programme of reform was going to answer. The expectation was that his younger brother Constantine (1779–1831) would prove more amenable to constitutionalist demands. However, Constantine passed up the chance to succeed as Czar: the election of his younger brother as Nicholas I (1796–1855) on 24 December 1825 prompted rioting and rebellion on the streets of St Petersburg and in the higher echelons of the army. Inspired by the reforms of earlier czars, what Lenin was later to call Russia's 'aristocratic revolutionaries' wanted the introduction of a constitutional monarchy.

Nicholas had Alexander's autocratic instincts without any of his reformist leanings. He was frank in his admiration for Prussia and its military-bureaucratic state – in 1817, he had married Charlotte of Prussia, daughter of King Frederick William III. As far as the radicals were concerned, he had to be stopped. Hence the *Dekabristy*, or 'December Uprising', a coup attempt by some of the most distinguished officers of the imperial guard. The 'Decembrists', as they became known, wanted constitutional reforms and an end to serfdom, state censorship and arbitrary actions by the police.

Nicholas was resolute and ruthless and dealt speedily with the Decembrists: some were hanged and others sent into exile in Siberia. His position secured, he set about realizing all the revolutionaries' worst fears in a reign of despotism and fear.

CARNAGE IN THE CAUCASUS

The great event of the latter part of Alexander I's reign had been the invasion of the northern Caucasus in 1817 – ostensibly a policing action to stem incursions by raiding tribespeople on its southern borders. As with earlier conflicts in this area, however, Russia was also pursuing a long-term policy of expansionism into what it saw as essentially uncivilized territories, which needed to be brought to order. It was also seeking a safe buffer with the Ottoman Empire and Persia to the south.

To some extent, Russia's programme of pacification was to be advanced by peaceful policies of economic development. In clearing forests, building roads and establishing towns down here, they simultaneously enriched these countries and weakened the hold of local warlords. However, like other European colonists, they did not consult the populations on how their lives were to be improved, and reacted with savagery whenever they were crossed.

Below: Russian troops cross the Abyuka River in the course of their campaign in the Caucasus: imperialism under the pretence of peace-keeping.

In Chechnya and Dagestan, whole villages were burned and entire communities wiped out in retribution for rebel actions. Sunni Muslim consciousness had been rising in the region since the days of Sheikh Mansur, which only stiffened Caucasian resolve.

WHAT'S IN A NAME?

Aleksey Yermolov (1777–1861) had taken charge of operations in the Caucasus in Alexander I's name, but he relied on his own to establish Russian sway. 'I want the terror of my name to guard our frontiers more effectively than any chains or fortresses,' he told his Czar. He got his wish; it is less clear that Alexander I got his – the Caucasus was to cause trouble for a long time yet.

Above: Aleksey Yermolov had some success in putting down resistance in the Caucasus, but the resentment his cruelty caused was to prove enduring.

The first problem was the Circassian question: this people, living along the northeastern coast of the Black Sea, had followed Sunni Islam for centuries, but had been radicalizing recently. Czar Nicholas I deemed the Circassians a problem, and demanded that the problem be removed. Quite what he meant is debatable – and is still debated to this day.

The Czar certainly wanted them moved out of 'his' Empire, and wasn't concerned how they might feel about being forcibly relocated: many tens of thousands were shipped across the Black Sea and dumped on the Ottoman and Persian coasts. Just as many seem to have been killed on the ground in Circassia itself, however – either because they resisted or because it saved the Russians trouble. Today, then, if there is a Circassian question, it is whether this atrocious episode should be seen as ethnic cleansing that got out of hand or remembered as a deliberate genocide.

Above: A blazing
Turkish fleet lights up the
sky above Sinop ... But
this was to be as good as
it got for Russia in the
Crimean War.

CRIMEAN CATASTROPHE

Nicholas's 'strength' as a ruler can hardly be disputed; his
effectiveness is another question. Russia's ramshackle greatness
was thrown into an unforgiving light by the Crimean War. This
was largely caused by Nicholas's arrogance (although France was
to be involved, this time as a Russian nemesis). The period from
1800 to 1850 had seen Russia's population just about doubling,
from 35 million to almost 70 million, but there had been no
corresponding economic growth.

Nicholas showed no sign of appreciating these realities: he
thought his thunderous commands should be implicitly obeyed.
Angered by the fact that the Ottoman Turks, under pressure from
Paris, had made France sovereign authority in the Holy Land, he
resolved to apply some pressure of his own. In 1853, accordingly,
he invaded the Ottoman Empire's Danube principalities of
Wallachia and Moldavia. As Nicholas had anticipated, the
Ottomans prepared for war; however, so too did France and
Britain, who Nicholas had expected to remain neutral.

It was with their backing, then, that the Sultan demanded Russia's immediate withdrawal. Nicholas's refusal sparked conflict. Soon there was fighting on the Danube and the Black Sea; the Imperial Russian Navy smashed the Ottoman fleet in the harbour of Sinop, northern Turkey. With things apparently going Russia's way, in the weeks and months that followed the focus of the fighting shifted towards the Crimean Peninsula.

The Western powers, supported by public opinion in their own countries, were not prepared to tolerate this expansion of

SCOURGING THE SERFS

AS WE'VE SEEN, SERFS were their landlords' property and open to abuse of every kind. Some landlords would beat their serfs in their own dining rooms in the presence of their guests. Punishment records from Petrovskoe, southeast of Moscow, in the 1830s, show that thrashing with birch rods was part of the daily work routine. 'For

work offenses,' writes historian Steven L. Hoch:

serfs received the fewest lashes, an average of thirty-one blows. For the theft of wood or timber, the serfs got an average of thirty-four lashes; for negligence during watch, which usually meant a theft had taken place, thirty-eight lashes; for intentionally letting animals feed in the fields or for serious theft, forty lashes; and for insolence or fighting, forty-nine lashes.

Landlords could be prosecuted for abuse, but the threshold was extremely high and, to all intents and purposes, they could beat serfs and rape their women pretty much at will.

Left: Legal prohibitions of abuse were laughed at by landowners. Russia's serfs often suffered appalling treatment.

Russian power. They declared war on Czar Nicholas I; France granted the Sultan a large loan, and from the spring of 1854, they were actively intervening in the struggles. By June, Britain had built a major supply base in the outskirts of Istanbul.

DOSTOYEVSKY DOES TIME

IN NOVEMBER 1849, THE famous Russian novelist Fyodor Dostoyevsky was condemned to death for engaging in seditious activities. He and his friends had been meeting regularly for what we might call a 'book group' – though the titles chosen had all been critical of the workings of the Czarist state. Sentenced to be killed by firing squad, the 'conspirators' were marched out on to St Petersburg's Semyonov Square on the night of 23 December. They were lined up ready for the troops to fire when a letter from the Czar arrived commuting their death sentences.

Dostoyevsky and his friends were exiled to Siberia, to a *katorga* prison camp outside the town of Omsk. Dostoyevsky was to spend the next four years there. 'The level of a society's civilization can be judged from a visit to its prisons,' he was famously to say: by that standard, Russia was not to score high. 'All the floors were rotten,' he recalled:

Filth on the floors an inch thick; you could slip and fall. The little windows were so covered with frost it was almost impossible to read at any time of day. An inch of ice on the panes. Drips from the ceiling; draughts everywhere. We were packed like herrings in a barrel. … We shivered all night. Fleas, lice, and black beetles by the bushel…

Left: Dostoyevsky during his Siberian exile – a formative time for him as writer and thinker.

OUTGUNNED, OUT-SUPPLIED

The armies of Britain and France might have been much smaller than Russia's, but they were much better armed, equipped and trained. The Russian musket had an effective range of 200m (656ft); that of their opponents was five times greater. Russian infrastructure barely existed: south of Moscow, there was no railway network, which meant moving everything along dirt roads by horse-drawn wagons. The Western powers, supplying their forces by sea, could bring in reinforcements or materiel at three weeks' notice; the Russians needed three months for the – far shorter – overland journey. So chaotic was the logistical situation, and so wretched the conditions, that one in three Russian soldiers never even made it to the front.

It was in the course of the Crimean conflict that Tolstoy had many of those first-hand experiences of war that were to be recycled and reimagined for the scenes of Borodino and other battles in *War and Peace*. (He had also spent time in the Caucasus.) In *Sebastopol Sketches* (1855), Tolstoy described his experiences more directly in lightly fictionalized form:

But again the sentry has shouted in his loud, thick voice, 'Mortar!'; again there is a shriek, and a bomb bursts, but with

Above: The Battle of Inkerman (5 November, 1854) was bloody on both sides, but there was no doubt in the end that the Russians came off worse.

this noise comes the moan of a man. You approach the wounded man, at the same instant as the stretcher-bearers; he has a strange, inhuman aspect, covered as he is with blood and mud. A part of the sailor's breast has been torn away.

The only real winner was disease. Cholera had raged since the summer, inflicting appalling casualties on both sides. Typhus too was rife; indeed, many of those supposedly killed by wounds sustained on the battlefield were really victims of the inadequate treatment they received and the squalid conditions in which they were kept.

ALEXANDER, WHO APPEARS TO HAVE LEARNED FROM HIS FATHER'S MISTAKES, IS NOW LOOKED ON AS THE GREAT LIBERATOR OF HIS COUNTRY.

In the end, the Western allies won – or perhaps it is more true to say that the Russians lost, defeated at last by the endless attrition of their forces. Well over 100,000 died on the Russian side.

THE EMANCIPATOR

The death of Czar Nicholas and the succession of his son Alexander II (1818–81) gave Russia a face-saving pretext for entering into peace negotiations. At the Paris talks of 1856, the Ottomans agreed to the equal treatment of Muslims and Christians in their empire, in return for which Russia would renounce the claims that Nicholas had made to a 'guardianship' role. Russia was additionally required to withdraw from the Danube delta and the Black Sea was declared a neutral zone: neither Turkey nor Russia was permitted to have coastal defences or warships there.

Alexander, who appears to have learned from his father's mistakes, is now looked on as the great liberator of his country. As Russia reeled in defeat, he seized the moment to introduce a raft of far-reaching reforms. One of the first was his abolition of serfdom (1861), which freed thousands from generations of semi-slavery.

Further changes followed. New institutions were created to look after law and order and public administration at local level in the countryside, till then the responsibility of the aristocratic

Opposite: Russian forces make an ignominious retreat from Sebastopol after the Allied capture of this vital naval base.

Above: The pomp and splendour surrounding the talks at the Congress of Paris (1856) cast a favourable light on what was really a Russian humiliation.

landowners. Elected assemblies, or *duma*, were developed to administer the cities: all classes were in theory represented here. The reality was that these bodies were dominated by the wealthiest merchants. Even so, it was clear that Russia was changing.

These internal reforms went hand in hand with a new opening up to the West, no doubt encouraged by Alexander's marriage with the German princess Marie of Hessen-Darmstadt (1824–80). The Czar helped foster traffic in goods and ideas alike, relaxing import regulations and softening censorship. His introduction of a unified national budget was not only good economic housekeeping, but helped stimulate investment from abroad. He welcomed Western capital, which underwrote the construction of a gigantic railway network across Russia, in turn promoting industrial development. Engineers, sent abroad to train, returned once qualified and workshops and factories sprang up in the rapidly growing towns.

FROM TENSION TO TERROR

Russia might have been better for Alexander's reforms, but it wasn't necessarily happier. Enlightened as he might be, Alexander was as despotic as any of his predecessors: all his reforms had been imposed; he was changing Russia from the top down. There was no sign of real democratization and, given a taste of progress, the people only clamoured for more – particularly the educated middle class and the new and fast-growing industrial proletariat.

The situation was volatile and, as peaceful protest became ever more widespread, a more sinister sort of opposition began

DARK TRADITIONS, GRIMM TALES

THE 19TH CENTURY WAS generally a time of rising nationalism in Europe. Across the whole range of Germany's fragmented states, a sense of shared identity had found itself in the fairy tales of the Brothers Grimm. Jacob (1785–1863) and Wilhelm (1786–1859) had scoured the furthest-flung corners of the countryside for their folktales. Firmly rooted in tradition and comparatively untouched by literary convention, these stories seemed to represent German culture in a 'natural' and 'unspoiled' state.

So it was in Russia, where, inspired by the example of the Brothers Grimm, Alexander Afanasyev (1826–71) published his *Russian*

Fairy Tales. More than 600 stories in all, appearing between 1855 and 1867, these tales told Russians how rich a folkloric heritage they had, and underlined the darkness of that heritage. Grimms' fairy tales had brought their share of shocks, but Russia's folktales hinted at a national history rooted in negativity and cannibalistic self-destruction. How else to explain the prominence of the old witch-woman Baba Yaga, who lived in a hut that walked on chicken's legs, and who killed and ate any hapless children who came her way?

Left: Baba Yaga sweeps across the sky in a giant mortar, carrying a pestle along with her witch's broom.

emerging. A new breed of radicals felt that only revolutionary change would give the people what they needed, and were prepared to bring about this transformation by any means necessary. The modern scourge of 'terrorism' arguably made its first appearance at this point, the Czar narrowly escaping assassination in April 1866. After a second attempt on his life during a visit to Paris for the World Exhibition of 1867, Alexander abruptly halted his reform programme.

Understandably, perhaps, he had taken the attempts on his life quite personally. The reformer reinvented himself as a reactionary. The Poles had long been aware of his autocratic side: he had begun his reign by warning them that they should have 'no dreams'. Their uprising of 1863–4 had been savagely put down; the Czar had been almost as ruthless in the repression of other national movements within his realms. Now, however, Alexander came consciously to count himself among the company of conservative monarchs. It was this realization that

Below: Polish patriots rise up against Russian oppression, 1863: they were very soon to be savagely put down.

lay behind his formation of the Three Emperors' League in 1872. This informal grouping with the emperors of Austria-Hungary and Germany was explicitly aimed at organizing resistance to the reform that the rising middle class was calling for across just about the whole of Europe.

In some ways, autocracy suited Russia: certainly, significant gains were made in foreign policy as Alexander's armies made conquests in Central Asia and the east. Tashkent, Bukhara, Samarkand and Khiva were all taken, and the Ottomans were defeated in the Russo–Turkish War of 1877–8. But the revolutionary spirit was at large; the assassination attempts went on and, in 1881, Alexander was killed by a bomb in St Petersburg thrown by a member of the revolutionary group *Narodnaya Volya*, 'The People's Will'.

Alexander's younger brother ascended the throne in his place. Unlike Alexanders I and II, Alexander III (1845–94) dispensed with the initial dabblings in democratization and set out his stall as a reactionary from the start. This was hardly surprising, given the circumstances of his succession, but was not the wisest decision. *Narodnaya Volya* made him a target too, and although their claim to represent the people's will may have been presumptuous, the desire for an opening up of Russian society

Above: Alexander II's assassination (1881), as represented in a contemporary engraving: the anarchist's bomb set off a panic in official circles.

was growing. Alexander set himself solidly against this wider movement. One of his first actions was to oversee the foundation of the *Okhrana* ('Guard Section'), a highly secretive department of the Interior Ministry that investigated and suppressed political dissent.

SOMEONE TO BLAME

The desire for democratic reform was growing, but so too – and in direct response to this restlessness – was the sense that social stability and the old order were under threat. As ever (and not only in Russia), such anxieties found a focus in the Jews. One of the conspirators in the late Czar's assassination, Gesya Gelfman (1852–82) was Jewish (even if she had rejected her religious and cultural background), so obviously the Jews collectively had to expiate her crime. Within weeks of

Above: Alexander III as he wished to be seen by his subjects, his hand on the hilt of his sword, ready to deal decisively with any opposition.

Alexander III's accession, pogroms had erupted across Russia – even in the Pale of Settlement. Only a few dozen people were actually killed, but several hundred girls and women were raped, and many thousands of men were beaten. Many families were burned out of their homes and businesses and in some cases expelled from the towns where they'd been living.

Russia's Jews were used to being scapegoated. What made the present round of pogroms so unsettling was the sense of official tolerance – if not collusion. The Czar himself, reactionary as he was, is not believed to have sympathized even secretly with the rioters: he saw no upside in outbreaks of disorder of this kind. But he didn't sympathize with the victims either: indeed, his response essentially acknowledged that their very presence was a provocation. Alexander's 'May Laws' of 1882 restricted the Jews' economic and professional opportunities still further while also confining them completely to urban areas – even within the Pale

Opposite: Jews gather nervously in a city street in the aftermath of one of the state-sanctioned pogroms of 1906.

of Settlement. The smaller village-sized *shtetls* (and the whole way of life that had evolved there) were consequently off-limits to them now.

ANTI-SEMITISM AS USUAL

Alexander died in 1894, to be succeeded by his son Nicholas II (1868–1918). Nicholas did not have an auspicious start to his reign: when, in a Moscow park, a crowd celebrating his coronation stampeded, more than 13,800 people were killed and thousands more were hurt. Meanwhile, the pogroms went on. Indeed, they worsened: some 2000 Jewish men and women were killed in attacks between 1903 and 1906. Unlike his father, Nicholas appreciated the upsurge in anti-semitism, seeing it as a useful thing for Russians to have an alien element to bond against.

Nicholas needed an internal enemy, as by 1905 he had lost the Russo–Japanese War over Manchuria and Korea, which he had seen as potential windows on the Pacific. Japan had been

WHAT MADE THE PRESENT ROUND OF POGROMS SO UNSETTLING WAS THE SENSE OF OFFICIAL TOLERANCE — IF NOT COLLUSION.

modernizing rapidly over several decades now, and its land and naval forces were well armed and organized. Defeat to them was no disgrace, especially for Russian forces that, although officially fighting from their own frontiers were operating thousands of miles from anywhere they could call home. But Japan's swift rise had taken the world by surprise: from the Western perspective, it was still a quaint, semi-medieval 'oriental' nation, so Russia's defeat meant a major loss of face. Given the impossibility of pushing Japan around, the search was on for a softer 'Asiatic' victim. Who better than that old standby, Russia's Jews?

FAKE NEWS

THE *PROTOCOLS of the Elders of Zion* purported to be the record of a meeting at which a committee of leading Jews had plotted the takeover of the world. Their representatives, they agreed, would extend their influence slowly but surely through the various arms of the economy, the media and the state, securing control over the mechanisms by which the whole world lived.

In reality, this was the work of the Czar's *Okhrana*. Always 'too good to be true', in the sense that it exactly corresponded with the anti-semites' long-standing assumptions, it was proven to be a forgery in 1921. By then, however, it already had all the traction that it needed.

Being revealed as a forgery did little to prevent the influence of the *Protocols*

PROTOKOLY
ZE SHROMÁŽDĚNÍ
SIONSKÝCH MUDRCŮ

Left: Tragically, the *Protocols* has proven to be one of the most influential publications of modern times.

on anti-semites. Despite its public exposure (in the London *Times*), it was believed implicitly and widely circulated around the world. Hitler was its most notorious reader. The industrialist Henry Ford (1863–1947) had thousands of copies printed and distributed in the United States. The *Protocols* has its fans in far-right groups in Europe to this day. And, a more recently recruited readership in the Muslim Middle East, where it provides the semblance of a contextual frame through which the policies pursued by the state of Israel may be viewed.

REVOLUTION IN REHEARSAL

Russia's defeat in East Asia precipitated a further collapse of confidence in the establishment, from the military top brass to the Czar. The state bureaucracy was included in this contempt, as were the leading lights of the new industrial economy. Popular discontent was nothing new in Russia, but the failure of those in charge to bring home victory from the field of war and secure prosperity at home led to unprecedented insubordination. Strikes and demonstrations burst out.

The government's response was uncompromising: on 'Bloody Sunday', 22 January 1905, 1000 hungry peasants, led by a priest, who had marched on St Petersburg's Winter Palace to present a petition pleading for assistance, died when soldiers opened fire. The demonstrators had been peaceful and unarmed; they were far from being a threat to the Czar, who wasn't even in St Petersburg at the time.

Above: Bloody Sunday, 1905, marked the end of any pretence that the Czar was his people's protector. Protesters flee as soldiers (in the foreground here) open fire.

There could be no pretence now that Nicholas II was on the people's side. Russia's rural poor had always seen their Czar as a father figure, kind and protective – even if his sight was sometimes blinded by corrupt and cynical 'advisers'. The urban proletariat was more sophisticated – and hence maybe more cynical. Even so, there was something new in the way in which both the Czar and his office were becoming objects of general hatred. The feeling was mutual. Over the next two years, more than 14,000 people were executed for sedition and over 75,000 imprisoned and exiled.

OVER THE NEXT TWO YEARS, MORE THAN 14,000 PEOPLE WERE EXECUTED FOR SEDITION AND OVER 75,000 IMPRISONED AND EXILED.

Official brutality only spurred on the resistance. Demonstrators marched on ministerial offices and threw up barricades. There were mutinies in naval bases – and, most notoriously, on the Battleship *Potemkin*. Typically, the nationalist backlash targeted not the well-armed mutineers or militants but defenceless Jews, of whom up to 3000 were slaughtered in a renewed round of pogroms.

CONSTITUTIONAL COMPROMISE

The Czar was forced to cave, to the extent of agreeing to let an Imperial Duma (an elected assembly) run Russia, while he took on a more symbolic role. Although anything but happy, he might at least have found consolation in the knowledge that the Social Democrats were deeply disappointed too. They disdained the bourgeois liberal elite to whose interests the October Constitution of 1906 was most obviously geared, but couldn't carry the people with them in resisting what appeared to be a victory.

By now, Nicholas had more pressing problems within his own family, as his son and heir Alexei (1904–18) was gravely ill. His royal pedigree (not only his father but his mother Alexandra of Hesse were of 'royal blood', the latter a granddaughter of Britain's Queen Victoria) had brought with it a less welcome legacy. The Czarevich suffered from haemophilia and the failure of Europe's finest doctors opened the door, in the Empress Alexandra's desperation, to less conventional healers

BOLSHEVIKS VS MENSHEVIKS

RUSSIA'S SOCIAL DEMOCRATS – Marxist revolutionaries – had at the conclusion of their Second Party Congress in London in 1903 divided into two factions. The *mensheviks* ('those of the minority'), led by Juliy Martov (1873–1923), had wanted a loose and open party structure in which individuals would be able to speak their minds. Vladimir Ilyich Ulyanov (1870–1924), better known now by his codename *Lenin* ('Man of Iron') had led the majority *bolshevik* faction with his call for the party to be a tightly knit group of dedicated and strictly disciplined revolutionaries.

The difference may sound superficial, but much more than style was at stake. The communists' great prophet, Karl Marx (1818–83), had never seen much scope for activism. Although it was historically inevitable that the revolution would come, it would come about through capitalism's economic contradictions. The proletariat would throw off its chains when it was good and ready. Lenin's belief was that if history needed a nudge from him

and his comrades then so be it: they would do what was needed to bring about the revolution. Given the importance of that final goal, individual opinions had to take second place to party discipline: it would all be worth it in the end.

It wasn't strictly Marxist, perhaps, but it made a sort of sense: were they really supposed to sit back and let things take their course while Russia's working people languished in hunger and in cold? That said, the idea that a small elite could make the revolution happen was obviously a recipe for dictatorship in a way that Martov's prescription might not have been.

Right: A dramatically-lit Lenin rallies the Russian people in their revolutionary moment.

– and some decidedly less respectable ones, such as Grigory
Rasputin (1869–1916).

A POWERFUL PRIEST

A self-styled priest and spiritual healer, Rasputin was revered by
those who fell under his spell. They didn't see the venal drunk
and violent sexual sleazebag others did. The harder her husband
and his advisers tried to talk her out of her emotional dependence
on Rasputin and his promise of a cure for her son, the more
determined Empress Alexandra became to keep him by her.

In fairness, Rasputin's enemies discredited themselves in their
efforts to discredit him. There is no real evidence that he had
carried out peasant weddings for free in return for first-night
privileges with the bride, nor that he'd been arrested for exposing

Below: 1906, and
Nicholas II presides
over the opening of the
Imperial *Duma* (elected
assembly), but his
concession was much too
little, much too late.

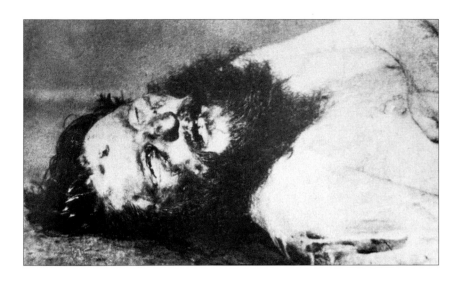

Left: Dead, at last: Rasputin's influence had seemed immensely threatening to the Imperial family – but vastly greater dangers were of course lying in wait.

himself in a Moscow restaurant, and Alexandra would have been in a position to know those things. She would also have been in a position to know the truth about the widespread gossip that she and this weird, unkempt mystic were adulterously involved.

The truth is that, so sacrosanct was the status of the Imperial household and the importance of the Czarina within it, Alexandra was sullying her family and country by having as much contact with the 'healer' as she did. If her relationship with Rasputin was not sexually scandalous, it was still outrageous in other ways. A foreigner by birth – and from a Germany with which by 1914 Russia would be at war – Alexandra's responsibility as empress was to keep her head down and her behaviour unexceptionable.

In December 1916, a group of nobles led by Prince Felix Yusupov (1887–1967) and Grand Duke Dmitri Pavlovich (1891–1942) resolved to assassinate Rasputin, fearing that he would bring down the Romanovs and imperial rule at large. Inviting him to Yusupov's home, they plied him with poisoned cakes, which when he finally ate, seemed proof against. When he was then shot in the chest and again failed to fall dead, their fear grew, although a further two shots finally put paid to him. Such was Rasputin's reputation that the story grew in the telling, his uncanny resilience an ill omen for an imperial Russia apparently hurtling towards its own death.

5

SOMETHING BETTER?

Successive military disasters were steadily eroding the authority of the Czarist system, but could Russians find a replacement that would really meet their country's needs?

'EVERYONE LIVES for something better...', says Luka, a character in a play by Maxim Gorky (1868–1936). Written in 1902, and set in a hostel for the homeless in a provincial city, *The Lower Depths* portrays the plight of Russia's poor. Perhaps it is only now in hindsight that its title can also be seen to sum up where Russia was as the new century began. Western countries such as Britain, Germany, France and the United States were forging ahead economically, leaving Russia mired in backwardness, industrial development barely stirring.

Gorky's real surname was Peshkov; his pen name means 'bitter', which suited his anger at the social injustices he saw. Like Luka, though, he looked forward to better things for his fellow citizens in a way that might seem dangerously sentimental now. The years that followed brought only further defeats and humiliations for Russia – and further degradations for the country's poor.

Opposite: The Bolshevik leader Lenin addresses a meeting of the Second All-Russian Congress of Soviets at Petrograd's Smolny Institute, 1917.

Above: Maxim Gorky's radical idealism made him a natural enthusiast for the Russian Revolution, though he became increasingly uncomfortable with the communist way of thinking.

WAR AND RENEWAL

When, in 1914, Russians saw an opportunity for national recovery in the 'War to End War', they jumped at the chance – just as others had across Europe, from Albania to England. Embarrassed at the German name Peter had given their capital, St Petersburg, they renamed it 'Petrograd' in the Russian style. The whole country was rediscovering itself, it seemed.

Here, as elsewhere, though, that initial all-over-by-Christmas high gave way gradually to disappointment and disillusion. The conflict quickly subsided into a static slugfest fought between troglodytic armies trapped in trenches, killing optimism and idealism on all sides. But the events of recent years – in everything from the Russo–Japanese War to the political arena – had left Russia's troops disproportionately disenchanted. Soon they were voting with their feet, deserting at a rate of up to 30,000 men a month.

CONFLICT AND COMMUNISM

At the same time, Russia's left-wing radicals had made support for the war a litmus test. Socialists said that ordinary people had no economic or political interest in what was really a power struggle between rival groupings of the international elite. A bayonet, they said, was 'a weapon with a worker at both ends'. What they didn't say was that a deserter was a weapon for the left. But their activists were there in force, stirring up dissent within the ranks.

Even so, sufficient Russian soldiers stayed in their posts to be cut down in their thousands in a series of hopeless offensives.

By the beginning of 1917, 700,000 Russian soldiers had died; a quarter of a million more were wounded. And there were hundreds of thousands of domestic disasters for those they had left behind in what were worsening conditions at home.

COMINGS AND GOINGS

Food shortages during the war hit hard. Workers in essential industries were angry at exploitative conditions, and striking freely; an atmosphere of mounting crisis reigned. In March 2017, Czar Nicholas stepped down, fearing that he would only be pushed if he didn't. He left an enormous vacuum. The so-called 'February Revolution' brought in a provisional government, but this was denounced as 'bourgeois' by the left. Lenin led this opposition, returning home from exile in the West by train and ferry via Helsinki. A crowd of supporters welcomed him at Petrograd's Finland Station. The provisional government tottered and fell, but its replacement that July by another one led by Alexander Kerensky (1881–1970) did not satisfy the all-or-nothing left.

> BY THE BEGINNING OF 1917, 700,000 RUSSIAN SOLDIERS HAD DIED; A QUARTER OF A MILLION MORE WERE WOUNDED.

Left: April 1917: Lenin's arrival at Petrograd's Finland Station after his years of exile was to become an iconic moment in the Soviet story.

Kerensky saw himself as a socialist – and indeed met all the customary standards, calling for collective ownership of the economy and government by workers' councils (or *soviets*, in Russian). However, he had not signed up to Lenin's programme. For the Bolsheviks, he was another namby-pamby liberal, offering 'bourgeois revolution'. Even so, they kept quiet, and Lenin went back to Helsinki to lie low for the time being.

Lenin returned in October 1917, when an attempted coup by conservative military officers led by General Georgiyevich Kornilov (1870–1918) prompted another political crisis. He and his Bolsheviks marched on Petrograd's Winter Palace, where the provisional government was holed up; crewmen of the cruiser

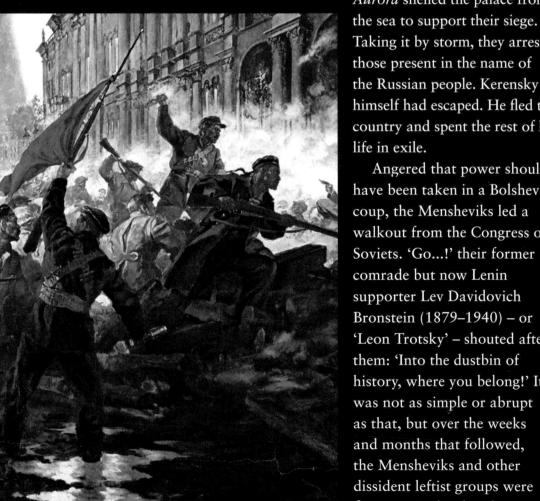

Aurora shelled the palace from the sea to support their siege. Taking it by storm, they arrested those present in the name of the Russian people. Kerensky himself had escaped. He fled the country and spent the rest of his life in exile.

Angered that power should have been taken in a Bolshevik coup, the Mensheviks led a walkout from the Congress of Soviets. 'Go...!' their former comrade but now Lenin supporter Lev Davidovich Bronstein (1879–1940) – or 'Leon Trotsky' – shouted after them: 'Into the dustbin of history, where you belong!' It was not as simple or abrupt as that, but over the weeks and months that followed, the Mensheviks and other dissident leftist groups were first marginalized within

government, then they were expelled
from it completely.

In the meantime, on 3 March 1918,
Russia's new government signed the Treaty
of Brest-Litovsk, extricating it at last from
World War I – albeit at the price of giving
up the Baltic States, Ukraine and much of
the Caucasus to the Central Powers.

'WE ARE NOT UTOPIANS...'
The first few months of communism were
a festive time in Russia. Famous artists
such as Marc Chagall (1887–1985) and
Wassily Kandinsky (1866–1944) were asked
to establish a new art for this new age of
infinite human possibility. However, as
envisioned by Lenin at least, communism
was an austere, puritanical creed. This
carnival of creativity couldn't last.

Marxism was 'materialistic' in the strict
sense of not accepting the existence of what
might be seen as belonging to the spiritual or sentimental realms.
There was no God, then; nor any place for 'idealism' in their
scheme – even if it was the revolutionary's overriding purpose
to change this world for the better. Even when, in the first flush
of Soviet triumph, the new government claimed ownership of
all private property on behalf of the people, took over all bank
accounts and nationalized industries and businesses, handing
control (at least ostensibly) to their workers, they maintained that
they were making Russian society more rational, not 'kinder'.

But the Bolsheviks were not utopians in another, more sinister,
sense, making no secret of their willingness to do whatever
it took to take and maintain power. In December 1918, for
example, Lenin established the *Cheka*, the Soviet secret police.
Its first head, Felix Dzerzhinsky (1877–1926) left no doubt of his
force's purpose: 'We stand,' he said on taking up his post, 'for
organized terror.'

Above: Happy to be
feared, Felix Dzerzhinsky
made no secret of his
belief that Bolshevik rule
should be imposed on
Russia at whatever cost.

PAYBACK TIME

WHEN WE LOOK BACK at the biographies of Bolshevism's movers and shakers, from Lenin himself to men like Zinoviev, Trotsky, and Josef Jughashvili or 'Stalin' (1878–1953), it isn't difficult to see how a lack of empathy might have entered in. Lenin's older brother, Alexander ('Sasha'), had been executed for his part in plotting the assassination of Alexander III. They all had to know the risks of the life they chose.

It wasn't just the fear, but the paranoia it brought with it: the *Okhrana*'s agents and informants were everywhere. Not just in Russia but abroad, where the revolutionary-on-the-run was compelled to lead a cloak-and-dagger life, constantly vigilant, suspecting any kind action or friendly face. They had been schooled by their mentor Marx to see nationalist identity as an aspect of 'false consciousness', one of those snares by which the capitalist system secured the attachment of those it would exploit. By necessity spending so much of their lives on the move, staying in safe houses in Zurich, London, Paris, Helsinki and Vienna, they would end up with a certain detachment from their home country, and from the people they nominally represented. The long evenings they spent in ideological wrangling encouraged a dry and analytical view on human politics even as their peripatetic existence fostered a feeling of rootlessness.

And, of course, they hated those who had for so long hated and hunted them. Once they won power, there was no stopping them.

The *Cheka* rounded up supposed saboteurs, class enemies and capitalist spies in their tens of thousands. While the *katorga* camps of the old regime had opened their gates with the Revolution, they were soon being redesignated as 'corrective' labour camps. 'No mercy for these enemies of the people, the enemies of socialism, the enemies of the working people!' Lenin wrote. 'War to the death against the rich and their hangers-on, the bourgeois intellectuals; war on the rogues, the idlers and the rowdies!'

In hindsight, there has been a temptation to see the Soviet Union's early history as a story of Lenin's benign idealism being hijacked by the monstrosity of Stalin. Thinking of the latter's insane violence, it is easy to see why. But such a narrative would have surprised Lenin himself almost as much as it would his victims: idealism, benignity and utopianism had no place in his scheme. The big-name artists soon left Russia for the West.

TERROR, RED AND WHITE

Lenin's ruthlessness was by no means unwarranted: the Czar's supporters had shown no compunction about killing. Although the language of condemnation was quickly debased, 'capitalist lackeys' and 'reactionaries' did exist. Moreover, they could call on support from abroad; the British statesman Winston Churchill (1874–1965), for example, had said that the 'infant' of Bolshevism should be 'strangled in its cradle'. To this end, he dispatched several thousand British troops, while a similar contingent was sent by France, to assist 'White' forces fighting for the Czar (or, at least, against the Bolsheviks: the 'Whites' actually represented a broad spectrum, from diehard monarchists to liberals and even dissident left-wingers).

A full-blown civil war resulted. The 'Whites' at one time controlled extensive areas of southern Russia and the Ukraine

Below: Commissar for War Leon Trotsky rallies his Red Army forces. The Revolution plunged Russia into civil war.

Above: The Imperial Family makes the most of the scant Siberian sunshine at Ipatiev House, Yekaterinburg, a few days before their execution in 1918.

and had a powerful presence in Siberia and East Asia. Their strength threatened to grow as members of the 'Red' Army deserted and in many cases went over to the other side. They continued the work of earlier nationalist extremists, carrying out pogroms and killing suspected leftists. Up to 300,000 are believed to have been killed in all. They themselves sustained terrible casualties fighting against the Reds: the losses were horrendous on both sides. By the time the Communists finally prevailed in 1923, seven million Russians had been killed in all.

Meanwhile, the fight had continued on the home front: in autumn 1918, an assassination attempt had been made against Lenin. In response, the *Cheka* led the crackdown that the Communists themselves called the 'Red Terror'. The 'enemies of the Revolution' had to be 'annihilated', said leading Bolshevik Grigory Zinoviev (1883–1936). They must be made to 'tremble', Lenin said. He certainly gave them reason to: over the next few years, at least 100,000 people were executed and hundreds of thousands sent into Siberian exile.

FAMINE...AND MORE TERROR

It was 19 years after the success of his play *The Lower Depths*, Maxim Gorky caught the attention of the world with another publication. This was not a play or novel but an open letter, calling on the international community for assistance for those afflicted by the famine ravaging Russia. 'The corn-growing steppes', he wrote, 'are smitten by crop failure, caused by the drought. The calamity threatens starvation to millions of Russian people.'

THE FALL OF THE ROMANOVS

IF THE WORKERS WERE banding together in solidarity, might it not have been expected that Europe's crowned monarchs would as well? It was King George V (1865–1936) who ruled out the Romanovs being granted a safe haven in England. His government agreed with some reluctance, and some resistance from Labour and Liberal politicians, but the king put his foot down, fearful of provoking a 1917-style revolution in his kingdom. In the aftermath of the Easter Rising in Dublin (1916) and major strikes and breakdowns in public order on 'Red Clydeside' and in Liverpool, George was afraid that his subjects would want to expel him.

Instead, stranded in Russia, Nicholas II and his family found themselves in an impossible position politically – though materially very comfortable – at residences near Petrograd and then, further east, outside Tobolsk. Their situation worsened after the October Revolution: they were reduced to (effectively punitive) military rations, deprived of their servants, then moved beyond the Ural Mountains to Ipatiev House in Yekaterinburg.

Although the Czar seemed confident that he and his family would be saved by the intervention of 'friends' abroad, they had become an embarrassment to Europe's beleaguered ruling houses, and to their traditional supporters in the conservative wing in politics who no longer wanted to be associated with what seemed a losing cause. As for the Bolsheviks, they could hardly have afforded to show mercy: the endurance of this family would be a perpetual spur to counter-revolutionary insurgencies.

On the night of 17 July 1918, at Ipatiev House, the Czar and Czarina Alexandra and their children were executed by a firing squad. Their executioners were gripped with terror as the young princesses – initially at least – failed to fall and die, protected by the pearls and jewels that they had sewn inside their bodices for safekeeping.

Left: The scene of the crime. It was in this room that the Czar and his family were shot.

Scientists today would be slower to blame the drought for the famine of 1921–22, although they would agree with Gorky's suggestion that 'war and revolution' had reduced Russia's 'resistance to disease and its physical endurance'. But the effects of a policy of collectivization, indiscriminately and unsympathetically imposed, had made a difficult situation impossible. If the Revolution had been Russia's attempt to find its 'something better', in Luka's terms, it was hard to see how it could be viewed as a success.

CLOBBERING THE *KULAKS*

The instincts of the Bolsheviks were to push ahead regardless and then look for a scapegoat when that went wrong. The 'reactionary

Below: Scenes like this from 1921 became gloomily familiar through the following decades as famine was first caused, then arguably weaponized, by the state.

elements' seeking to bring the soviets down weren't just old-time aristocrats or urban intellectuals, it seemed. They also included the grasping, self-interested peasants who (it was widely believed) had been hoarding grain in hopes of seeing its value rise. These *kulaks* – wealthier peasants and small farmers – were held up as public enemies.

> THE INSTINCTS OF THE BOLSHEVIKS WERE TO PUSH AHEAD REGARDLESS AND THEN LOOK FOR A SCAPEGOAT WHEN THAT WENT WRONG.

No matter that the more than 50 million hectares of land confiscated from the *kulaks* withered away under inexperienced and incompetent collective management. The crucial thing was their tight-fisted avarice and their implacable opposition to social progress. Communism's leaders were clever people, but this strange combination of high-flown intellectualization and the broadest and most boorish personal prejudice would characterize Soviet thinking from this time on.

ECONOMIC ANTAGONISMS

Lenin's government had relied on a tough economic policy of 'War Communism' to see what was now the Union of Soviet Socialist Republics (USSR) through the difficulties of its inception. It did the job, but by the time the Civil War was over, the country was in a ruinous state. A 'New Economic Policy' was clearly called for. This was the name that Lenin gave to what he hoped would only be a transitional stage on the road to a fully socialist economy but which critics in the capitalist world have seen as his unconscious acknowledgement of the realities of economics and of human nature.

The policy had more in common with capitalism than anyone might have expected, given the radicalism of the Bolsheviks' rhetoric up till now. It offered a mixed economy, in which state-owned enterprises were geared to making profits and privately owned companies could work alongside them, under the ultimate supervision of the state. In the countryside, the rhetoric against peasant-proprietorship was reined back: those who did the work of growing Russia's crops could do so with the knowledge that, if they worked hard, they might make a real cash profit.

6

TEMPERING THE STEEL

In Stalin's Soviet Union, the brave new future was built in brutality and bloodshed. Sheer terror held sway across the 'workers' state'.

'TONYA, CUT yourself loose and come to us. Let's work together to finish with the bosses.' This is the climactic romantic moment in one of the classic works of Soviet literature, *How the Steel was Tempered*. 'I would be a poor husband to you if you expected me to put you before the Party,' an impassioned Pavel Korchagin continues; 'For I shall always put the Party first.' An epic of the Civil War, this novel appeared in serial form between 1932 and 1934; a book-length edition followed in 1936. That same year, its author Nikolai Ostrovsky (1904–36) died. The novel had been based loosely on his own life.

Opposite: 'Let's hit the target on the state grain procurements fully and on time.' Soviet citizens went through life surrounded by urgent exhortation of this kind.

EMOTIONAL ENGINEERING
The title *How the Steel was Tempered* seems almost comical now in the closeness with which it conforms to the oddly industrialized aesthetics of the 'socialist-realist' school. Ever since Lenin had (in 1920) famously characterized communism

as 'Soviet power plus the electrification of the whole country', economic development had been a vital adjunct of patriotic pride. Technology was invested with enormous prestige. Stalin (whose own codename, of course, meant 'Man of Steel') informed an assembly of Soviet authors that 'the writer is the engineer of the human soul'. He evidently meant this as high praise. The author had the honour of being an industrial worker in his or her own right, contributing to the construction of the great new state. Loyal writers such as Ostrovsky took pride in using language to underline that consciousness; hence the comparison between the processes of human life and growth and those of making steel.

Russian writing of the kind officially sanctioned in Soviet times was paradoxically conservative (at least with a small 'c') in turning its back on the modernist experimentation characteristic of 'bourgeois' literature of the time. Writers such as Marcel Proust (1871–1922), Virginia Woolf (1882–1941) and James Joyce (1882–1941) had reinvented the novel, but the soul's engineers rejected 'formalism' of this kind. Instead, employing narrative techniques developed by the European novelists of the 19th century, they set out a moral and intellectual order in which Soviet values were proclaimed. When the sufferings of the workers and their struggles against their oppressors were accurately depicted (the 'realist' element), the reader would inevitably be led to an apprehension of socialism's truth.

Below: A happy, ideologically-compatible couple – and who are we to sneer? Nikolai Ostrovsky poses here with his beloved wife and comrade Raisa.

OPTIMISM TO ORDER

Socialist-realist writing has been derided as banal, yet Ostrovsky's novel enthralled millions of readers. If that is no guarantee of its artistic merit, it suggests that it did possess some compelling human hold, perhaps

in the sense such novels gave of writer, reader and society as a whole pulling together with a common purpose – and in an uplifting faith that a better life could be achieved. It was certainly easier to find optimism in the pages of such novels than it was in Soviet reality.

Lenin admitted that the New Economic Policy represented a major climbdown, although he had thought it justified in pursuit of the greater goal. Many in his party were opposed, however; a faction led by Trotsky saw it as an outright betrayal of the Revolution. Others, including Stalin, sided with Lenin in accepting it as a necessary evil. The split was unresolved when Lenin died in 1924, leaving his post as Party Chairman (and de facto Soviet Premier) unfilled.

'TOO CRUDE'

'I trust no one. Not even myself,' Stalin said. He knew what he was talking about. Lenin had warned his friends against letting

Above: *How the Steel was Tempered* took on talismanic status: a Red Army unit kept this copy (with author's notes) throughout the whole of World War II.

Above: Russians turned out in their tens of thousands to see the body of Vladimir Lenin carried through Red Square to its resting-place in January, 1924.

Opposite: 'The Reality of this Programme is Real People: It's You and Me,' insists a poster (1931) which shows Stalin marching with the workers' rank and file.

Stalin seize power. His ruthlessness had its place in the Party, but not at its helm, he said. Someone 'more tolerant, more polite, and more attentive towards comrades, less capricious, etc' was needed for the position of General Secretary. Stalin was 'too crude' for this, he said. These were wise words, but they weren't to prevail. Not only did Stalin win his leadership; he claimed to have done so as Lenin's friend and designated successor.

Against the wishes of Lenin's widow, Stalin had the late leader's corpse embalmed and installed in a great mausoleum outside the Kremlin in Red Square. The 'personality cult' he wove around this shrine – and the hundreds of statues he had set up in cities across the Soviet Union – gave Stalin proprietorship over the Lenin legend. It underlined his own legitimacy as the great revolutionary's successor and would (he hoped) cast Lenin's mantle of socialist glory over him.

STEELY BUT SLIPPERY

Stalin may have been crude, but he was cunning too. Even as he lauded Lenin's legacy, he revised it. Quietly ditching the internationalism that had been at the heart of Marxist ideology, he claimed Leninist legitimacy for his own view that the Soviet Union should limit its aims to achieving 'Socialism in One Country'.

NOT ONLY DID STALIN WIN HIS LEADERSHIP; HE CLAIMED TO HAVE DONE SO AS LENIN'S FRIEND AND DESIGNATED SUCCESSOR.

In fairness, this policy reflected the views of ordinary Russians, who favoured priorities that put their country first. Stalin, himself a Georgian, also showed a more realistic understanding of the identities of the Soviet Union's different ethnic groups – however ruthlessly he was to trample these when it suited him.

Stalin was also evasive in the way he quietly disowned vast tranches of the Leninist project that he himself had vociferously supported in the great man's lifetime. Under Stalin, the *kulak* was joined in the USSR's league table of hate figures by the '*NEPman*' – the opportunistic shyster who had enriched himself under the (Lenin-launched and Stalin-supported) New Economic Policy. The USSR, Stalin insisted, had lost its way under the NEP and needed to get back on socialist track and build a highly centralized state-directed economy.

AN ECONOMIC OVERHAUL

Stalin believed that the USSR was 50 to 100 years behind the great Western economies. 'We have to close that gap in ten years or we will be crushed.' That target set the schedule for the two Five-Year Plans he now set out. The first, starting in 1928, would tackle the biggest and most basic structural problems in the economy.

Soviet agriculture in its entirety would be collectivized: big, rationally organized units taking full advantage of the economies of scale and mechanization would replace small family farms and peasant-plots. In its early years, the Revolution had confiscated

INCORRUPTIBLE EVIL

LIKE LENIN, LEON TROTSKY (1879–1940) had benefited from comparisons with Stalin. Anyone so bitterly disliked by that monster couldn't be all bad, we tend to think. Indeed, the man born Lev Bronstein into a wealthy Jewish family in the prosperous port city of Odessa, on Ukraine's Black Sea coast, does command respect for his intellectual rigour and his political commitment.

Stalin had served prison time and substantial spells of exile for his beliefs as well, however: sincerity doesn't in itself make anyone a saint. All the evidence is that, in Trotsky, the great 'what might have been' of Soviet history could well have been just as bloody and tyrannical as it turned out. First as Lenin's right-hand man in the Bolshevik faction, then, from 1918, as Commissar for the Red Army and Navy in the Civil War, Trotsky had shown himself a cold and ruthless commander.

These were virtues in Trotsky's book: an eager student of the French Revolution, he had a special admiration for Maximilien Robespierre (1758–94). The so-called 'Incorruptible' had presided over the Revolutionary Tribunals of 1793–4,

Above: Leon Trotsky in his revolutionary pomp.

the vast estates of the big aristocratic landowners, but this hadn't impacted much on what should have been the Soviet 'breadbasket' in the 'black earth' regions of the south.

Industry would be reorganized along the same lines, large-scale state enterprises replacing the mid-sized factories and small local workshops that had gone before. Again, such a reordering should allow enormous efficiencies and accelerations in production, catapulting the country into the 20th century.

Progress was only possible if everything was done systematically and on the utmost scale. Modernization itself would have to be industrialized – like literature. Soviet society

sending hundreds of political dissidents to their deaths. Robespierre would have revelled in the cruel reputation he has had in his posterity. 'Terror', he claimed, was 'nothing more than speedy, severe and inflexible justice'. Likewise, Leon Trotsky wore his ruthlessness as a badge of courage and integrity. He simply did not believe in compromise.

That unswerving steadfastness was to be Trotsky's undoing: he had clashed with Lenin several times during his lifetime, but the late leader had recognized his qualities throughout. Stalin feared his abilities, though, and did his best to discredit his main rival, smearing him as another 'enemy of the people'. This was despite the fact that Trotsky had been the most outspoken opponent of Lenin's New Economic Policy, which Stalin now condemned, although he had supported Lenin at the time.

By 1927, Stalin had forced Trotsky

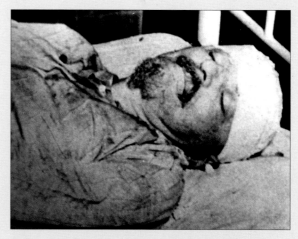

Above: Trotsky's assassination was a warning to wayward leftists around the world.

out of the Communist Party; by 1929, he had forced him to leave Russia. Even in exile, Trotsky was a thorn in Stalin's side; finally, in 1940, he had him assassinated. A Spanish communist, Ramón Mercader (1913–78), went to Trotsky's home in Mexico City's Coyoacán district and killed him with an ice axe to the head.

„К КОНЦУ ПЯТИЛЕТКИ КОЛЛЕКТИВИЗАЦИЯ СССР ДОЛЖНА БЫТЬ В ОСНОВНОМ ЗАКОНЧЕНА".
(И. СТАЛИН)

„..РАБОЧИЙ КЛАСС СОВЕТСКОГО СОЮЗА ТВЕРДО И УВЕРЕННО ВЕДЕТ ВПЕРЕД ДЕЛО ТЕХНИЧЕСКОГО ПЕРЕВООРУЖЕНИЯ СВОЕГО СОЮЗНИКА-ТРУДОВОГО КРЕСТЬЯНСТВА".
(И. СТАЛИН)

had to be fashioned into a machine for making the future; people had to make themselves its moving parts. There was no place in such a scheme for individualism or freedom of expression: the good citizen put society, and socialism, first.

'DEKULAKIZATION'

The Soviet leadership's resentments against the *kulaks* became intensely emotional. 'We must smash the *kulaks*, eliminate them as a class,' said Stalin. The leaders had clashed with the *kulaks* from the start; sturdily self-reliant, they had been slow to adapt to the social template the communists wanted to fit them into.

Lenin had sparred with the *kulaks* in the first months of the Revolution. From 1930, however, their liquidation was official Soviet policy. The *kulaks* were to be sent to the gulags or forcibly removed from their familial lands. Of those expelled (at a conservative estimate, almost two million in the first 12 months), some were sent to smaller, less desirable, plots in nearby districts; others were shipped to unsettled areas in western Siberia, the Urals or Kazakhstan.

Stalin's suspicion of these small farmers takes us back to Russia's history of the carnivalesque. Like the top-hatted plutocrat, the caricatured figure of the backward but grasping peasant perhaps had a place in the cartoon art of the Party press. Historical and immediate experience alike had made Russia's country people conservative and resistant to change – certainly when change was imposed upon them by city-dwelling strangers. They were also undoubtedly selfish – if that's how we want to characterize the desire

Opposite: 'By the End of the Five-Year Plan Collectivization Should be Completed,' this poster (by the Latvian artist Gustav Klutsis (1895–1938) enthuses.

Below: The rural Revolution marches on beneath a banner reading 'We as Collective Workers Will Eradicate the *Kulaks*...' in 1932.

to do the best for themselves, their families and perhaps their neighbours, rather than for some remote and abstract state.

In the overwhelming majority of cases, neither were the *kulaks* wealthy. Most were very poor, although they had occupied their own land and enjoyed some limited autonomy. This meant they could conduct themselves with a certain waywardness when asked to change their practices against their will.

FROM FOLLY TO FAMINE

The hostility to the *kulaks* caused chaos and carnage. Many were killed by angry officials for refusing to move or for 'cheating' the system by slaughtering livestock to prevent it being taken from them for the collective farms.

When, inevitably, the collective farms, dragged down by unwilling workers or inefficient practices, failed to produce the

CANAL TO NOWHERE

THE IDEA OF A ship canal linking the White Sea with the Baltic, cutting out a hazardous sea-passage round Norway's Northern Cape, had obvious appeal both as a waterway, with all the logistical advantages it would bring, and as a prestige project, a showcase for the Soviet achievement under Stalin's first Five-Year Plan.

The canal was built entirely by convict labour, largely with picks and shovels and little mechanized support. The bulk of those who worked here – over 100,000 in all, from 1931 – came from the ranks of Russia's political prisoners. The wastage rate among those forced to toil to breaking point and beyond on its construction has been contentious, but at a conservative estimate 25,000 died.

After its triumphant opening in 1933 (three months ahead of schedule), the canal was little used over the decades that followed. The waterway linked a chain of lakes with stretches of canalized river and newly cut canal. In their eagerness to meet their deadline, engineers had skimped on the depth of the channel, which was never really adequate for the sort of seagoing vessels for which the canal was ostensibly being built.

Ultimately, then, it showcased Soviet economic capacities in quite the wrong way, highlighting a strategy geared more to presentation than achievement. It depended too on the dragooning of vast numbers of unwilling labourers into work in which they felt no individual investment or commitment. Corners were inevitably cut.

miracle harvests Stalin's economic strategists had confidently predicted, the peasants were the first in line to starve. Officials took their appointed share, regardless of whether an area could sustain the toll. Indeed, those small farmers who failed to meet their quotas were fined in kind, so those who had not produced enough grain to start with were immediately deprived of the little they had.

Far from intervening to alleviate these problems, the authorities in Moscow ignored the famine. They flatly denied that anything was amiss, spurning offers of assistance from the international community while trumpeting the success of the First Five-Year Plan. Indeed, the USSR exported food throughout this period. The hard currency it earned abroad could help build industry: what did it matter if a few more million died?

A boy of 11 in 1933, Mykhaylo Naumenko later recalled what happened on the collective farm where he and his family lived:

People became swollen, they died by the tens each day. The collective farm authorities appointed six men to collect and

Above: Officials uncover a cache of hidden grain beside a *kulak*'s home in Kurgansky, southern Russia. The 'guilty' parties could expect immediate execution or lengthy exile.

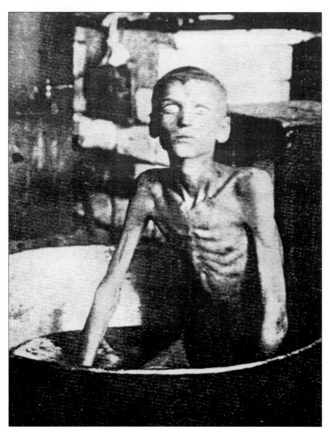

Above: The 'New Soviet Man' was to personify perfection in education, morality and physique … In the Ukraine, things hadn't got off to the best of starts.

bury the dead. From our village of 75 homes, by May, 24 houses were empty, their inhabitants all dead.

Pilfering, even of essential food, was seen as a crime against the state. Those caught, however piteous their hunger, were shot or sent to a labour camp: the penalty for taking a single handful of grain was a five-year term. Of the thousands crowded into cattle trucks and sent to the Arctic north or east to Siberia, 20 per cent would not even reach their destination. Few would live to complete their sentences: perhaps one in 50 at a generous estimate.

Most chose not to risk their lives or freedom and simply endured their situation, passing slowly and painfully through hunger to starvation. Up to 10 million people died, and in the most demeaning of circumstances, brought to the edge by their frantic hunger. 'People were eating cats, dogs…' recalled Antonina Meleshchenko, who went through the famine years in Kosivka, near Kiev:

In the Ros river all the frogs were caught out. Children were gathering insects in the fields and died swollen. Stronger peasants were forced to collect the dead to the cemeteries; they were stocked on the carts like firewood, than dropped off into one big pit. The dead were all around: on the roads, near the river, by the fences.

Mykola Karlosh described how her family and neighbours 'searched the fields for mice burrows hoping to find measly amounts of grain stored by mice.'

But the Five-Year Plan was sacrosanct: 'People died at work,' said Galina Gubenko, from Poltava, central Ukraine:

It didn't matter whether your body was swollen, whether you could work, whether you had eaten, whether you could –

you had to go and work. Otherwise – you were the enemy of the people.

Some officials sent to enforce the collectivization policy saw the damage they were doing and reported their concerns to their seniors. They were at best ignored, but they were often executed for their pains.

GENOCIDE?

Was this a cock-up or a conspiracy? It is hard to make the former suggestion stick given the determination with which Stalin's government pressed on long after the appalling human cost of this programme had become clear. If the latter, though, what kind of conspiracy was it? An excess of ideological zeal? Some historians have argued that there was an 'ethnic cleansing', even a 'genocidal', aspect to the campaign given that such a high proportion of its victims lived in what was then the Soviet Republic of the Ukraine. The Ukrainians in general have believed themselves singled out in what they call the *Holodomor* or 'terror-famine'.

Below: In the early days of Ukraine's *Holodomor*, a dead body on the street was still worth stopping for. As the weeks went by that was to change.

Stalin does seem to have disliked the Ukrainians – although there is a certain circularity to this argument given that he saw their republic as a nest of *kulak*-ism. He was not wild about Kazakhstan, either, where a similar agrarian system had held sway and where comparable casualties were sustained. Kazakhstan had only been part of the Russian Empire since the 1890s, however, and its farming people had generally been settlers from this time. They hadn't had time to develop the historic sense of national identity that Ukrainians had, and through which – inevitably – they filtered their experiences of the *Holodomor*.

REPORTS OF CANNIBALISM WERE RIFE, IN FACT. STATE POLICE GOT AS FAR AS PROSECUTING OVER 2500 PEOPLE FOR THIS CRIME.

Genocidal or not, the famine and accompanying repression took a sizeable chunk out of Ukraine's population. If Stalin and his supporters did not deliberately set out to kill millions of people, they took no heed of the harm they were doing when things went wrong. Indeed, their rhetoric was from the first so stridently aggressive, their prosecution of the plan so unswervingly deliberate, that it hardly makes sense to dispute their murderous intent.

There is no doubt that the dekulakization programme was driven by deep and visceral hatreds, even if these seem to have been more ideological and class-based than racial in origin. Signs of 'nationalist' feeling were indeed identified and steps taken to stamp them out, but this was more for the sake of socialist internationalism and social discipline. Dangerous 'nationalist' tendencies were detected even within the Party, its Secretary in Kharkov, in the Ukraine,

'EATING YOUR CHILDREN IS BARBAROUS'

'EATING YOUR CHILDREN is a Barbarian Act,' one official poster pointed out during the Ukrainian famine. Reports of cannibalism were rife, in fact. State police got as far as prosecuting over 2500 people for this crime – which suggests an actual incidence a great deal higher. Many of those prosecuted were parents who had ended up eating their own children: the strongest taboos were not proof against the ravages of hunger.

Historian Timothy Snyder (in *Bloodlands*, 2010) describes one police report as saying that 'Families kill their weakest members, usually children, and use the meat for eating'. Snyder himself notes the case of a mother who 'cooked her son for herself and her daughter'. In an orphanage in Kharkov, Ukraine, a group of children brought inside for protection against being attacked by adults, started to eat the youngest child, 'little Petrus', alive:

They were tearing strips from him and eating them. And Petrus was doing the same, he was tearing strips from himself and eating them, he ate as much as he could. The other children put their lips to his wounds and drank his blood. We took the child away from their hungry mouths and we cried.

Pavel Postyshev (1887–1939), reported. With evident satisfaction, he told Stalin that more than 100,000 members had been expelled – the vast majority executed by firing squad.

TOUGH LOVE

'Why did you beat me so hard?' Stalin is said to have asked his mother later in life. 'That's why you turned out so well,' she answered. The Soviet Union was to get the same tough love. Not that Stalin's repressive ways represented such a dramatic transformation. Russia had been plagued by secret police of one sort or another since the *Oprichniki* of Ivan the Terrible's time. As we've seen, the Czarist *Okhrana* had in December 1917 given way to a new set of secret police, the *Cheka*, who killed and tortured in the People's cause.

Towards the end of 1922, the *Cheka* became the State Political Directorate (or GPU), then, about a year later, the

Opposite: This statue, and the candle-memorial behind it in Kiev, commemorate the famine of 1932–3. Behind them is a *Holodomor* museum.

THE GRIM GULAG

Above: Transported *kulaks* were set to work in gulags.

THE SOVIET GULAGS – penal labour camps – were notorious, although strictly speaking there was really only one. The word – an acronym of *Glavnoye Upravleniye Lagerej* ('Main Administration of Labour Camps and Settlements') – referred to the system as a whole, which encompassed hundreds of camps and smaller settlements across the USSR. What we would call 'political prisoners' were held alongside every other kind of criminal.

As so often in Soviet historiography, the monstrosity of Stalin's conduct has left Lenin's looking a little pallid. He did not shrink from packing opponents off to prison camps, however. No fewer than 84 had been established by 1921, and Stalin expanded the system massively.

With so many different camps, and so many prisoners kept there (more than 100,000 were held by the end of the 1920s; many millions more would pass through the system over the decades that followed), their inmates' experiences might be very different. In some cases, the worst of the punishment was the fact of exile – although simply surviving the rigours of the Arctic and Far Siberia was hard enough, and those sent out there were often made to work as well. In many others, men (and women) endured nightmarish conditions crowded into insanitary camps, with unspeakable food and inhuman treatment. A good proportion were worked to death, in lumbering, mining, farming or in industrial labour.

All-Union State Political Directorate (OGPU). It was the OGPU that set up the gulag system. Even so, they were wound up in 1934, to be replaced by the NKVD ('People's Commissariat for Internal Affairs').

THE GREAT PURGE

The Soviet Union had never offered the most tolerant environment for political dissent: democracy did not mean disagreement, in Lenin's view. Rather, the communists had represented what they knew to be the best interests of the People, regardless of what the people wanted for themselves. What made the Stalin era different was the degree of distrust within the state and Party; the replacement of suspicion by rampant paranoia.

In 1934, Sergei Kirov (1886–1934) was assassinated. He had been head of the Communist Party in Leningrad. Who killed him isn't clear – some have suggested that it was done on Stalin's orders to provide him with the pretext he sought to stage a security crackdown. Whether he would have felt the need for an excuse is doubtful: either way, he lost no time in launching a major operation against what he regarded as subversive elements in Soviet society.

In the 'Great Purge', between 1936 and 1938, well over a million people perished; many more were imprisoned or exiled. Those

Below: Stalin stands beside Sergei Kirov's coffin – his own victim, it has been suggested. He certainly exploited Kirov's death to justify his purge.

branded bourgeois traitors or agents of Western imperialism included men and women till then held up as heroes of the Revolution: lifelong communists; even former friends of Stalin. No one was too loyal to hear the knock on the door in the small hours announcing the NKVD's arrival to whip them off for interrogation and torture; no one's career was sufficiently unblemished to place them above suspicion. Holding up under torture was seen as evidence of guilt, although so, of course, was confession. Those who cracked could at least be relied on

OBJECT OF ENVY

As ONE OF STALIN'S senior hate figures, Nikolai Bukharin (1888–1938) took on the role of a sort of right-wing Trotsky – although only by Bolshevik standards would he have been considered ideologically of the 'right'.

Bukharin had spent the six years prior to the Revolution in exile, dedicating his life to the overthrow of the Czarist state. His main offence thereafter appears to have been being brilliant, charismatic, charming and immensely popular with the Party membership. That would always make him seem a threatening presence to a man of Stalin's insecurity – as Bukharin himself confided to a friend:

It even makes him miserable that he cannot convince everyone, including himself, that he is a taller man than anybody else... Any man who speaks better than he does is doomed; Stalin will not permit him to live, for this man will serve as an eternal reminder that he is not the first, not the best speaker...Yes, yes, he is

Above: Bukharin, sporting a 'Lenin' cap, stands beside his leader Comrade Stalin in this picture.

a small, malignant man – or rather not a man but a devil.

From a leading position on the left, Bukharin had gradually moved to a more pragmatic stance. He had been a staunch supporter of the New Economic Policy and continued to call for a mixed economy after Lenin's death when the political situation changed. Arrested in 1937, he was accused of plotting to overthrow the Soviet government and executed after a show trial in 1938.

to furnish lists of 'co-conspirators' to be arrested and tortured in their turn. Many disappeared, never to be heard of again, although a few fortunate individuals would reappear later after years of exile in the east. Most were summarily shot: the army's firing range at Butovo, south of Moscow, became a firing range of a new and sinister kind during the Purge. Between August 1937 and October 1938, 20,000 people were executed and interred in mass graves at the Butovo complex. On one single day in February 1938, 562 people were executed.

The atmosphere was of total paranoia: every pronouncement was parsed, every utterance analysed. The wrong word or phrase – even the wrong overtone – might signal sympathy with Trotskyism or Bukharinism (see box). The pressure was on to denounce others before they could demonstrate their loyalty by denouncing you – although the risk remained that under torture they would confess to a conspiracy involving you and bring you down. Neighbours – even family members – informed on one another.

Above: Vladimir Putin stands beside the Orthodox Patriarch Aleksey II at this ceremony commemorating those who were executed and then buried at Butovo.

Right: By 1936, even 'Bolshevik Royalty' like Grigory Zinoviev had fallen on tougher times – as this official mugshot shows.

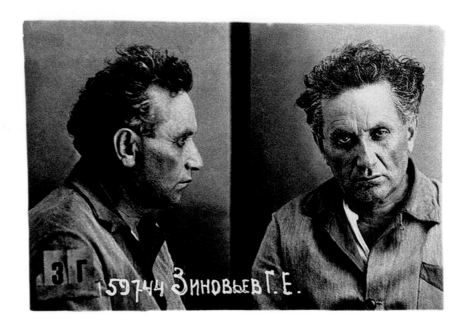

THEATRE OF CRUELTY

Most of Stalin's victims disappeared with barely a ripple, bundled off by goons in the middle of the night to be imprisoned, tortured and then (mostly) shot. A select few, however, were arraigned for their alleged offences at ceremonial 'show trials', which played an important part in the propaganda of the state. This latest version of the Russian carnival paraded its pantomime villains before a horrified yet spellbound public, underlining the external and internal threats the Soviet Union was up against and the need for vigilance to continue, with all that meant in suspicion and the never-ending round of denunciation, arrest, torture and death.

A series of such trials were held in Moscow between 1936 and 1938, the defendants a cast of communist heroes of the recent past. Gregory Zinoviev (1883–1936) had been a close confidant of Lenin back in the day, and a pillar of the Politburo ever since. Lev Kamenev (1883–1936) had been another hero of the Revolution and the Civil War, but as Trotsky's brother-in-law had been living on borrowed time.

What shocked a watching Russia (and a horrified international audience) was the way the accused made apparently unforced confessions of their treasons. All the evidence is that

Opposite: Genrikh Yagoda illustrates the fickleness of fate within the Stalinist universe: he went from being a trusted henchman to a reviled victim within two years.

these admissions had been coerced by torture and blackmail (threats were made against their families).

The rise and fall of Genrikh Yagoda (1891–1938) illustrates the feverishness prevailing at the time of the Great Purge, and the speed with which events could move. As Stalin's NKVD head, he had been behind the action against Zinoviev and Kamenev. This was a personal triumph for Yagoda – but therefore a dangerous omen for his future. The kudos he had earned transformed him from a trusted henchman into a present threat; within two years, he had his own show trial and was executed by firing squad.

MOST OF STALIN'S VICTIMS DISAPPEARED WITH BARELY A RIPPLE, BUNDLED OFF BY GOONS IN THE MIDDLE OF THE NIGHT.

RED RUST

By 1933, the Soviet Union was busy with its Second Five-Year Plan. Along with further improvements to the country's communications infrastructure of roads and railways, machine-tools production was expanded to seven times its former level. As previously, however, heavy industry had priority – and especially steel production, which was successfully doubled over the duration of this plan.

Steel needs tempering to make it true. While the output of the Soviet Union's steelworks soared, the quality of what was made was for the most part fairly low. As for the more metaphorical steel of Soviet men, women and society, that was being fiercely tempered in the fire of Stalin's fury. In theory, the dictator was burning away the impurities, improving the quality of Russia's social metal. As time went on, though, it became hard to see this happening. In attacking those echelons of the Party and wider society where those

with the talent and experience to pose a threat were to be found, his actions corroded the quality of the state.

PACT WITH THE DEVIL

In the military, in industry, in the bureaucracy, in just about every area of society, those with enterprise and talent were being liquidated. It did not bode well for Russia's ability to deal with the threat then looming from Nazi Germany in the West. Hitler's 'Thousand-Year Reich' was notionally to find its necessary *lebensraum* ('living space') on the steppes of Slavic Europe, where German settlers would produce an abundance of food by conscripting subhuman Slavic labour.

Stalin saw the dangers but, having by his policies of repression robbed his country of any satisfactory means of defending itself, felt forced to enter a non-aggression pact with Hitler in 1939. This gave Hitler the run of western Poland while allowing the Russians to take the east – and Baltic states such as Latvia, Lithuania and Estonia – without any objection from the Germans.

CREATIVITY AND COMPULSION

'ONLY IN RUSSIA IS POETRY RESPECTED,' wrote Osip Mandelstam (1891–1938): 'it gets people killed'. His words were prophetic; his own satirical scribblings of the dictator led to his exile with his wife and fellow-writer Nadezhda (1899–1980) and then later to his death.

Stalin's thuggishness did not preclude a serious, if sadistic, interest in the nation's cultural life. He had written poetry and painted to a creditable standard himself. But his insistence that, like Ostrovsky's Pavel Korchagin, the good communist would always 'put the Party first' was bound to ossify his aesthetic sense.

It is hard to imagine a modern head of state bothering to go to see a new contemporary opera and then contribute an anonymous review to the nation's press. In a way it is impressive that Stalin felt compelled to. But it's disturbing too that the great composer Dmitri Shostakovich (1906–75), whose *Lady Macbeth of the Mtsensk District* (1936) was the work in question, condemned for its 'formalism', should have been thrown into such a career-derailing spin of confusion and of fear. Ultimately, he was able to rehabilitate his work with the authorities – but, many felt, at immense creative cost.

This also gave Stalin's admirers in the Western left the most severe of shocks. They had bent over backwards to make excuses for earlier excesses, from the Ukrainian famine to the Moscow show trials – or explain them away as exaggerations (or even as complete fictions) of the capitalist ruling class. To see their hero carving up Eastern Europe with the diabolical German *führer* stretched their credulity to its limits.

Stalin was in his element, though, marking his occupation of Poland's eastern half by conducting a sort of preparatory purge. Just about the whole of the country's officer class was arrested, along with police officers, civil servants and assorted teachers, lawyers and generally educated individuals. On the orders of NKVD chief Lavrentiy Beria (1899–1953), they were taken to Katyn Forest, west of Smolensk, where more than 20,000 were shot and thrown into mass graves.

The Nazi–Soviet Pact had not fooled anyone. Its cynicism was clear for all to see. It had, however, bought Hitler time to start establishing his European empire in the West and Stalin much-needed breathing space. That said, no one could be completely surprised when, on 22 June 1941, the Germans attacked the USSR with history's biggest ever invasion force.

Above: The killing-ground at Katyn, where Poland's officer class was executed en masse in the aftermath of the Nazi-Soviet Pact of 1939.

7

'A WAR OF EXTERMINATION'

War is never pretty, perhaps, but the fighting that followed the German invasion of the Soviet Union had a special, apocalyptic fury all of its own.

THE DECISION by the Nazi leadership to deal with the 'Jewish Problem' once and for all led to the construction of a huge industrial infrastructure of murder. Death camps such as Auschwitz, Treblinka, Dachau and Bergen-Belsen have cast a shadow across post-war history. But to focus too closely on these massive complexes is to overlook the impact of the small-scale, low-key persecution in which peripatetic *Einsatzgruppen* ('deployment squads') roamed the countryside in the wake of the *Wehrmacht*'s main advance into the Soviet Union during Operation Barbarossa.

Opposite: A Soviet sniper stands in woodland, draped in camouflage material from a captured German tent, a year into Russia's War in Summer, 1942.

HOLOCAUST BY HAND

Wherever they went, *Einsatzgruppen* rooted out 'subversives' and rounded up 'undesirables', marching them out for summary execution. Often they had mobile gas chambers mounted on trucks to carry out their killings, although a bullet was often quicker and much cheaper.

Opposite: 'The last Jew of Vinnytsia', this snap was labelled in a German soldier's souvenir album ... S.S. *Einsatzgruppe* D dispatch victims outside this city in the Ukraine.

Below: This monument, in a memorial park outside Kiev, Ukraine, commemorates the tens of thousands of men, women and children massacred here at Babi Yar.

The Jews and Roma murdered elsewhere were joined in the Soviet Union by communist officials. One unit, *Einsatzkommando 3*, under the Swiss-born SS-man Karl Jäger (1888–1959) recorded over 135,000 killings over a five-month period in 1941 when the group was operating across Lithuania, Latvia and Belarus. The highest number of killings occurred in Kaunas, Lithuania: on 29 October, clearing a local ghetto of its Jews, the *kommando* murdered 9200 men, women and children in a single day.

One of the darkest moments of the Holocaust came at Babi Yar, a deep gully outside Ukraine's capital, Kiev. Here, on 29–30 September, Kiev's Jews, ordered to assemble with clothes and any valuables and money, were led to the gully's rim, relieved of their possessions and told to strip. A watching truck driver described the scene:

Once undressed, the Jews were led into the ravine... When they got to the bottom they were grabbed by members of the SS and local police and made to lie down on top of Jews who had already been shot... The corpses were literally in layers. A police marksman came along and shot each Jew in the neck with a submachine gun.... I saw these marksmen stand on layers of corpses and shoot one after the other.

RACIAL RAMIFICATIONS

The war in the East had always been one of race. As virulently as they hated its communist rulers, the Nazis hated Russia's 'Asiatic' aspect even more: German soldiers were told that they were taking part in the 'final confrontation' between civilized Europe and the East. Race and ideology shaded over into one another. In the words of Nazi historian Franz Lüdtke, German National Socialism and 'Jewish Bolshevism' could not co-exist: this was 'a war of extermination'.

Above: The Jewish prisoners here were rounded up by obliging units of the Lithuanian Home Guard after the Germans' invasion of their country.

In Nazi race theory, if the Jews were a disease, the Slavs were subhuman too. They were also to be slain without mercy where they weren't more useful being kept as slaves. In the weeks following this first few days of slaughter at Babi Yar, 100,000 further victims ended their days here. Along with further Jews, these included Russian prisoners of war and Roma.

Several hundred Ukrainian nationalists were also murdered. The Ukrainians were classed as Slavs, too. That said, their status seems to have been ambiguous; some were to find themselves somewhat redeemed for the Germans by their anti-Russian feeling, as well as their anti-semitism: local police officers helped with the initial arrest and liquidation of Kiev's Jews.

SADISTIC SYMBOLISM
The everyday stuff of war came with extra violence born of the conflict's racial aspect.

Villages were burned, their people massacred, and livestock and produce stolen or destroyed. Russian women were raped in their millions, with the encouragement of Nazi commanders who saw such actions as driving home the superiority of Germans over Slavs. Beyond their existence as living, feeling human beings, women assumed a symbolic significance (as they often have in war). Many Russian women were forced into brothels to service German soldiers on demand, their situation a daily reminder of their country's humiliation.

Many women fought as partisans – members of the Russian resistance militias fighting in the German rear. This was largely a matter of necessity: the Soviet Union was in a desperate plight. But it also served as part of a wider propaganda effort in which, liberated from old bourgeois gender roles, women were defending the Revolution, and Russia itself, on equal terms with men. Conversely, for the Nazis who captured them, Soviet women's sexual degradation and brutal murder was a representation of the wider subjugation of the Slavic race. Often these female soldiers were mutilated before they died – their breasts cut off, for instance – to show how they had unsexed themselves by bearing arms.

Gang rape was an important means of 'male bonding'. This kind of cruelty became a sort of social currency for the invaders. Far from feeling shame, German soldiers often boasted of these atrocities, taking snapshots to show each other and the folks at home. When these found their way into Soviet hands as Germans were killed and captured, they were shown in press and newsreel media, consciously heightening the fear of defeat or surrender, and the hunger for revenge.

RUSSIA ON THE ROPES

In the first few months of the German invasion in 1941, the contest was one-sided. The invaders carried all before them, their momentum moving them eastward at a rapid rate. Victories at Uman (July–August), Smolensk (July–September) and Kiev (August–September), and the encirclement of Leningrad (September), cost the Soviets dearly. Russian resistance was brave, but the Germans advanced in so much strength and with so much speed that their defensive efforts stood little chance.

By October 1941, though, that strength started to ebb. Marooned on the steppes just to the west of Moscow, the

Germans found that final push beyond them. Now they also faced the might of 'General Winter'.

Like Napoleon before them, they had found the length of their supply lines seriously challenging: winter clothing was one of the things they lacked. With temperatures of -30°C (-22°F) routine and levels of -45°C (-49°F) not unheard of, the Germans found themselves inadequately equipped. While a Russian counteroffensive made only patchy progress, that didn't alter the fact that the German advance appeared to have been stopped in its tracks; the tide of the conflict overall seemed to have turned.

ENEMIES WITHIN

The Russians' heroism was held against them by the Germans, who saw their willingness to fight to the death not as commendable courage but as evidence of an 'Asiatic' savagery; an animal obstinacy, even, essentially too bestial to fear death.

'BLACK MONTHS'

BY SEPTEMBER 1941, LENINGRAD'S population of 3.5 million had been swollen by an influx of refugees from the surrounding countryside. As eager as they were to take this important industrial centre and naval port out of the military reckoning, the Germans had no interest in taking responsibility for feeding so many people. 'We can', said a government directive, 'have no interest in maintaining even a part of this very large urban population.' They should, then, be allowed to starve to death.

That is very nearly what happened: just about encircled by German forces, the city's people suffered a siege that lasted for 872 days. Some supplies were brought in by winter across the frozen waters of Lake Ladoga. This 'saved' the city – although for many of its people it merely prolonged the death agony.

As hunger began to bite and fuel shortages shut down heating systems – winter temperatures regularly hit -30°C (-22°F) – people died at a rate of around 5000 a day. The starving were reduced to eating birds, rats and household pets, even boiling up soil in hopes of extracting nutrients. In some cases, they resorted to cannibalism. Meanwhile, the German bombardment continued, day after day. Not until the beginning of 1944 would the siege be lifted, by which time a million Soviet servicemen and well over half a million civilians had lost their lives.

Above: The successful
defence of Leningrad was
an extremely close-run
thing. German troops at
times got well within the
urban area.

Cold War historians in the West may have risen above this basic racism, but they too tended to play down the bravery of the Russian forces' fight. The product of a dehumanizing system that prioritized ideology over feeling and state loyalty over individual conscience, their soldiers – this Western view held – developed the insensate doggedness of the cog in the machine.

Communism's leaders would no doubt have loved to turn out automata like that, but there is no evidence that they did. When Soviet soldiers showed courage and commitment, they did so in the same way that those of other nations did, setting the lives of their comrades above their own.

However, not all Russian soldiers were heroes, and the authorities knew that. (They certainly did by the time 100,000 soldiers had surrendered in a single day at Uman.) One way they stiffened resolve was with Order 270, which made an officer's desertion, flight – or, really, anything less than a fight to the death – a dereliction of duty, automatically punishable by death. It was also a disgrace that would be visited on surviving family members in the form of exclusion from normal services and rights.

It was in officers' own interests to set the same standards

for their men. *Politruks* (political officers) had already been placed with each Red Army unit to help sustain morale, to report on where it was lacking and to lurk behind the lines to shoot deserters. Now such executions had the official backing of the law. The authorities did not beat about the bush: if a soldier's sense of patriotism and personal honour weren't enough to keep him in the front line, the fear of certain death if he sought to slip away generally convinced him to stay at his post and take his chances.

Above: Operation Barbarossa had caught the Russians badly unprepared. After the Battle of Uman (August 1941), Soviet prisoners were taken in their tens of thousands.

THE ROAD TO STALINGRAD

Simply outlawing defeat did not make the Red Army invincible: that became clear in the spring of 1942 at the Second Battle of Kharkov. Here, a Russian army was successfully encircled – and, despite Order 270, many men were captured. The conflict in the Soviet Union now became, in the modern cliché, a 'war for oil': Hitler was determined to push east to take the oilfields around Baku. That way he would secure supplies for his own armed forces' needs and – more important – rob the Red Army of its fuel. The city of Stalingrad (now Volgograd) first became an object of interest to the Germans as a strategic point in a movement to cut off the Caucasus.

The auguries all seemed good for the 270,000-strong German army that now advanced on the city by the Volga. The *Luftwaffe*'s air raids had left the city in ruins before they even arrived. Many thousands had been killed, but the

400,000-odd surviving civilians still cowering in the smoking shells of their old homes were a millstone around the necks of what was already an exhausted defensive force, outnumbered and outgunned by the army of Germany's General Friedrich Paulus (1880–1957).

'SURRENDER IS FORBIDDEN'

Both sides at Stalingrad were driven on as much by fear as by the will to win: 'surrender is forbidden,' General Paulus had told his soldiers. Likewise, the Soviet troops had received 'encouragement' from their political officers, quick to shoot not just deserters but wounded men 'malingering' or even those deemed over-hesitant in their fighting style. Besides, with the waters of the Volga at their backs, there was no realistic prospect of retreat, even if their superiors had been more forgiving.

The fight for Stalingrad – hand to hand, street by street and house by house – continued at a frantic rate: the lulls and the longueurs of most military campaigns were unable to take hold

Below: Stalingrad was the scene of some of the most ferocious combat of World War II: Germans and Russians fought for every building, every inch.

here, as men went crazy with the adrenalin and stress. Rations, ammunition and weaponry all ran low, only intermittently replenished by boat across the Volga. Men made petrol bombs with rags and bottles to tackle tanks and trucks, dug in inside drains and culverts and made nests in bombed-out factories and apartment buildings, ready to defend them with their lives. The trees were stripped of their leaves by bomb blasts and fire at the height of summer. In winter, the cold sent morale sinking on both sides.

The balance of the battle shifted gradually against the Germans. It took five months, but finally the Russian defenders threw the attackers back. The Russians eventually surrounded the Germans, prompting Paulus to forget his own instruction; on 2 February 1943, he announced an unprecedented and ignominious capitulation.

Below: Defeated German soldiers file into captivity at Stalingrad. Surrender was unthinkable, their Führer had insisted. But Paulus' army had at last run out of options.

Left: Over 8,000 tanks were involved in the fighting at Kursk, in the Summer of 1943, but infantrymen were killed in their tens of thousands.

CASUALTIES OF KURSK

A few months later (July–August 1943) came another Soviet victory at what is remembered as history's greatest ever tank battle: the Battle of Kursk. Infantry and artillery were involved as well, and their casualties were astronomical. Hundreds of thousands of Soviet soldiers are believed to have lost their lives. Far more Russians than Germans, indeed, although the Soviet censors kept the lid tightly on their losses at this and other battles of the time. The truth was, the Russian leadership felt they had any number of lives to throw into the fray against the Germans, especially now that things seemed finally to be going the Soviet Union's way. So great was the differential that some scholars have suggested that the Battle of Kursk was 'really' a German victory. If so, it was one that left them in headlong retreat.

FROM BAGRATION TO BERLIN

The following summer (June–August 1944), the Russians finally broke through the German centre with Operation Bagration. They had the initiative now, and started pushing rapidly westward – though still sustaining dreadful casualties. At the beginning of 1945, the East Prussian city of Königsberg fell after a four-day siege. By February 1945, it lay deep in

Above: Soviet soldiers atop Berlin's Brandenburg Gate raise their flag beside a battle-tattered chariot statue. The scene couldn't be more clearly symbolic if it tried.

Russian territory (where, as Kaliningrad, it still remains). The Eastern Front now extended from the Baltic to the Carpathian Mountains of eastern Romania. Six million Soviet troops faced around two million Germans along with some 190,000 Axis allies. In the vital central sector along the rivers Vistula and Oder, the Germans were still more comprehensively outnumbered and outgunned: 11 to 1 in terms of infantry, their generals estimated; 7 to 1 in tanks; 20 to 1 in heavy artillery.

RED REVENGE

The Russians had the new and heady sensation that their homeland had at last been saved and that the German wolf was being cornered in his lair. A savage spree of score settling began as years of pent-up anger were vented. If the rage of the Russian troops was easy to understand, it was also acceptable to their superiors in the communist government, who believed that – after dragging Russia into two world wars – Germany should not just be defeated but destroyed. Red Army reprisals were not just tolerated but tacitly approved. 'Soviet soldier,' a propaganda poster pointed out, 'You are now on German soil. The hour of revenge has struck.'

Terrible atrocities were committed, villages burned and refugees slaughtered, but what amounted to a programme of mass rape left the most indelible mark on the German population. It was inspired less by sexual frenzy than by a burning lust for vengeance and an overwhelming desire to degrade and humiliate the German nation.

The red flag went up over the Reichstag (the German parliament building) in Berlin on 30 April 1945. By that time, the Soviet Union had lost over 20 million lives. But the USSR had also emerged as one of the world's two 'superpowers' – a communist counterbalance to the capitalist United States.

CRYING RAPE

STALIN TOOK AN INDULGENT view of the Red Army's sexual depredations on its way through Germany and in Berlin itself (where 100,000 women and girls are believed to have been raped). Given what he had been through, it was understandable if a victorious Soviet soldier felt inclined to have a bit of 'fun with a woman' or to 'take some trifle', the dictator said. His political officers went further, urging their men on in a hideous attack that mirrored that of the Germans on Soviet women four years before.

To some in the Soviet Union, the earlier actions of the Germans would seem to justify this revenge rape now; officially (and even since the Soviet era

ended), Russian commentators have denied that it took place.

Well over half a century after the events themselves, and decades after the end of the Cold War, events like these remain contentious. Conservative historians and journalists in the West have arguably been much quicker to point the finger at the Red Army than at the *Wehrmacht* for this kind of 'strategic rape', although as far as the available evidence goes, the German troops' attacks in Russia were every bit as bad.

Germany has for decades been held accountable for the Holocaust. But has this attention come at the expense of more serious scrutiny of its ordinary soldiers' crimes?

СПАСИБО
РОДНОМУ СТАЛИНУ
ЗА СЧАСТЛИВОЕ ДЕТСТВО!

8

DROWNING IN FALSEHOOD

The end of the 'Great Patriotic War' meant a return to oppression–as–usual in Russia, Stalin's position only strengthened by his victory.

'THEY DON'T ask much,' said poet Boris Pasternak (1890–1960) of the officials running his native Russia: 'They only want you to hate the things you love and love those you despise.' They don't seem to have wanted his life, though, despite his open refusal to accommodate the socialist-realist aesthetic in his work. Neither did he accept its central moral assumptions that personal feeling and freedom were subordinate to society's needs and that the individual conscience came second to the greater good – as that was decided on by the Party.

To everyone's surprise (not least his own), Pasternak had survived the Great Purge, although he had publicly disassociated himself from the persecution of leading intellectuals and writers. Whether due to his international standing or some soft spot for him on Stalin's part, Pasternak was never arrested.

The purges continued, however, and ultimately came close to him. In 1949, his lover Olga Ivinskaya (1912–1995) was sent

Opposite: A boy in pioneer's uniform and a little girl with beautifully beribboned plaits bring flowers in thanks to their avuncular-looking leader.

to a gulag as a 'spy'. At the time of her arrest, she had been pregnant with his child, although she subsequently miscarried. Pasternak was convinced that she had been targeted as a warning to him. The introspective self-obsession his Soviet critics sneered at was in considerable part the creation of the scrutiny they had placed him under as the world watched to see what choices he would make. That sense of being under the spotlight becomes explicit in one of his most famous poems, where he imagines himself on stage playing Shakespeare's Hamlet:

I am alone; all round me drowns in falsehood.
Life is not a walk across a field.

TO THE VICTORS…FAMINE

The vanquishing of the Nazi threat brought immense relief in Russia, but did not do much for people's immediate quality of life. To some extent, this was true in the West as well: the only real consolation for the peoples of France and Britain through the long, drab years of 'austerity' was the knowledge that their situation was better than that of the Germans.

In Russia, however, the resumption of normal Soviet service was announced by a 1932–3-style famine and its complete mishandling in the now customary way. Hundreds of thousands died. Although many of those casualties were caused by starvation, others were shot by the authorities. Some were executed as saboteurs or agitators; others for supposedly misappropriating, hiding and hoarding grain – as before, wholesale scapegoating went on.

The truth that could not be admitted, despite overwhelming evidence, was that the agricultural system had once again

Below: Boris Pasternak was a major poet, but the adulation his work received in the West owed as much to political prejudices as to literary tastes.

LARA'S THEME

Olga Ivinskaya was later the model for Lara in Pasternak's famous novel, *Doctor Zhivago* (1957). Although rejected by Soviet publishers, a script was smuggled out of the Soviet Union and published in Italy. Its appearance was a major factor in the Russian writer being awarded the Nobel Prize for Literature in 1958, although – fearful of being refused readmission to Russia if he made the trip to Stockholm – he felt obliged to decline it.

Decisions of the Nobel Literature committee are often contentious and described as 'politicized'. Pasternak's prize undoubtedly was: CIA officials had lobbied to have him win the award, while the Russian establishment reacted with predictable rage. In truth, although Pasternak's importance as a poet cannot be doubted, this novel did not represent his finest work.

Above: The Communist Party paper, *Pravda* ('Truth') disapproves of the news of Pasternak's Nobel Prize.

Altogether, the affair illustrated the way in which the oppositions of the Cold War came to overshadow post-war cultural life more widely. Neither side missed an occasion to score points over or make mischief for the other. From theatre companies to academic journals, officials sought to direct artistic and intellectual life to the advantage of the geopolitical bloc to which they belonged.

proved lacking. As in the early 1930s, the Soviet Union continued hailing record production and continued exporting grain, even as the rural population starved.

THE IRON CURTAIN

With the war approaching its end, the 'Big Three' Allied leaders – Stalin, Britain's Winston Churchill (1874–1965) and America's Franklin D. Roosevelt (1882–1945) – had met to discuss the post-war settlement. The Yalta Conference, in the Crimea (4–11 February 1945), ended in agreement that Europe should be

РЕАЛЬНОСТЬ НАШЕЙ ПРОГРАММЫ
—ЭТО ЖИВЫЕ ЛЮДИ, ЭТО МЫ С ВАМИ,
НАША ВОЛЯ К ТРУДУ, НАША ГОТОВНОСТЬ
РАБОТАТЬ ПО-НОВОМУ,
НАША РЕШИМОСТЬ ВЫПОЛНИТЬ ПЛАН.

Above: The Great Leader, Comrade Stalin, at the head of a people on the march: a propaganda poster sings the praises of the Five-Year-Plan.

divided into Eastern and Western spheres, under the broad supervision of the victorious powers. It was to be an easy-going, arm's-length arrangement. Where was the sense, Stalin himself asked, in imposing communism on Catholic Poland? One might as well try to put a saddle on a cow.

Within months, the promised 'free' elections had been rigged in favour of pro-Soviet parties. In Churchill's words, an 'Iron Curtain' ran across the whole of Europe 'from Stettin in the Baltic to Trieste in the Adriatic'.

In addition to the Baltic states (annexed to the USSR as Soviet republics) and East Germany, what amounted to a Soviet empire extended across Poland, Czechoslovakia, Hungary, Romania and Bulgaria. While Yugoslavia, under Josip Broz 'Tito' (1892–1980), and the Albania of Enver Hoxha (1908–85) proved more wayward, the other 'People's Republics' were directly under Russian communist control: they were ruled with the same grim discipline as the Soviet Union itself. As signatories to the Warsaw Pact, they formed a military alliance (directly led by Moscow) against the North Atlantic Treaty Organization (NATO) of the West.

The Iron Curtain was to have its most nearly literal manifestation in the steel and concrete of the Berlin Wall.

REPATRIATION AND REVENGE

THE COSSACKS HAD ALWAYS been independently spirited and conservative. Many had fought with the White Army in the Civil War. Discriminated against in the decades since, some had seen the German invasion as an opportunity. Several tens of thousands had fought in the Axis' cause.

Many more Russian troops had fought with the Red Army in defence of their country, but – especially in those early months, when the *Wehrmacht* had been rampant – had been captured and held in POW camps. The thinking that had inspired Stalin's Order 270 prompted him to see such men as traitors, collaborators and (if allowed to return home) potential spies.

In their eagerness to keep Stalin on side, and ensure a safe and speedy passage home for any of their POWs who might end up in Soviet hands, the West's leaders at Yalta agreed to repatriate these Russian prisoners. With the war's end, anything up to two million were loaded into cattle trucks and sent east. Most went straight to Siberia; very few survived. One of any number of atrocities to be lain at Stalin's door, the episode has caused shame in the West as well: Britain and America were accessories in this crime.

Above: Soviet POWs sit around in a camp in Potschuz, USSR.

Although not constructed till 1961, it summed up the contradictions of Eastern Europe under Soviet rule throughout the entire Cold War era. Ostensibly built for East Berliners' protection, to keep western-originating dangers out, it was actually designed to keep would-be defectors in.

BY SPRING 1949, THE RUSSIANS COULD SEE THAT THE WHOLE ENTERPRISE WAS PROVING COUNTERPRODUCTIVE FOR THEM.

SOCIALISM IN MULTIPLE COUNTRIES

Stalin, as we've seen, had retreated from the internationalism that was conventional in Marxist thinking. Despite a rhetoric of brotherhood, he was in Eastern Europe essentially as an occupier. A further challenge to his views had come with the victory of Chinese communist leader Chairman Mao Zedong (1893–1976) in 1949, after years of fighting with

BERLIN AIRLIFT

THE EASTERN HALF OF Germany now had the title of 'German Democratic Republic'. How ironic this was became clear after the elections of 1946, when the people rejected a raft of communist candidates. The Soviets blamed interference by and agitation from the West. Tensions mounted till, in the summer of 1948, the Soviets placed a blockade on supplies to the western section of Berlin.

They were already chafing at having to acknowledge Western authority over the western half of Germany's conquered capital. It did indeed now occupy an incongruous position, a tiny bit of city, linked to the Federal Republic of (West) Germany by a narrow corridor. Stalin's intention was to make the maintenance of this connection increasingly difficult and irksome with the hope that the West would tire of it and find some face-saving way of writing off their stake in West Berlin.

As absurd as the situation was, its symbolic importance was considerable to both sides. When, in 1948, the Soviets started turning the screws, the British and Americans organized a major airlift to get supplies into the city. A quarter of a million flights carried everything from food and machinery to coal. By spring 1949, the Russians could see that the whole enterprise was proving counterproductive for them. Their blockade was lifted and normal rail services were restored.

he Nationalists in that country. The relationship was uneasy,
with nationalistic (and egotistic) factors alike creating tensions
between these two kingpins of world communism.

Stalin had done deals with Nationalist China in the 1930s
and during the recent war, for support against Japan. Mao
believed that the Nationalists' territorial concessions should be
cancelled in a spirit of socialist fraternity. Stalin agreed, but only
after a great deal of huffing and puffing. The two countries came
together in antagonism towards the United States and support for
Kim Il-Sung's communist North in the Korean War (1950–3).

The 'Cold War' between East and West was mostly only
allowed to flare up in proxy conflicts such as Korea and in
postcolonial liberation struggles like those of Malaya (from
1948) and French Indo-China (subsequently Vietnam). The
stockpiling of nuclear weapons on both the US and Soviet sides
had made the prospect of 'mutually assured destruction' (with
the apt acronym 'MAD') only too credible, so neither side

Above: Stalin lies in peace, prior to being placed beside Lenin in his Red Square mausoleum – and his subsequent removal under Khrushchev.

wanted to enter hostilities more directly. If the great enemy was the capitalist West, Russia's relations with China were still souring, rupturing completely in 1956 with the Sino–Soviet Split. This saw a division between the world's pre-eminent communist powers that would not be mended for ten years.

'BEAT, BEAT AND BEAT AGAIN'

Stalin's reign as Russia's 'Red Czar' continued to be characterized by a paranoia, which sometimes tipped over into insanity. One noticeable tendency of these later years was an ever more openly expressed anti-semitism. Officially, communism was internationalist in its principles, with no place for petty chauvinisms, but Party members were products of their own backgrounds and their times.

Anecdotal evidence abounds of Stalin making anti-semitic comments even in his early years. At the same time, the historical record shows him spearheading large-scale campaigns against discrimination of this kind. Hypocrisy? Preaching tolerance while practicing prejudice? Quite possibly. It is also conceivable that Stalin was ambivalent in a deeper and more complex way, capable of both bitter racist feeling and of more enlightened thought. As cruel as his purges had been, Jews had been statistically over-represented among their victims only to the extent that they had also been over-represented in the urban intelligentsia, and hence within the Party's ranks.

As age and failing health heightened Stalin's feelings of vulnerability, his paranoia grew more profound. In 1953, he had nine of his personal physicians arrested and tortured for allegedly taking part in a plot to poison him. 'Beat, beat and beat again,' he ordered his interrogators. Confessions were finally secured and the unfortunate medics charged. In the event, they were saved by Stalin's death. He was found on his bedroom floor at the *dacha* outside Moscow that he went to for breaks. A cerebral haemorrhage had killed him, though there was some question as to what had brought it on. It was probably natural causes, but rumours persisted that his deputy (and sometime NKVD chief) Lavrentiy Beria had poisoned him.

DEFECTIVE PERSONS

THE VERB 'TO DEFECT' (to leave one's country and seek asylum in another) seems loaded, derived as it is from the Latin *deficere*, 'to fail'. In the Cold War era, the term came to describe many men and women who fled west to escape from Soviet tyranny.

Stalin's own daughter was a defector: Svetlana Alliluyeva (1926–2011) caused a sensation when she sought sanctuary in the United States in 1967. In what became a tug of Cold War love, she was wooed back to the Soviet Union in 1984, before heading west again some years later.

Rudolf Nureyev (1938–93) was probably the world's most celebrated ballet dancer, a lead with Leningrad's Mariinsky Ballet, when he sought asylum while on tour in France in 1961.

Much later, in 1988, a whole family, the Ovechkins, hijacked an Aeroflot domestic flight in hopes of being taken to London to seek lasylum. Instead, under the pretence of making a refuelling stop in Finland, the pilot landed at a Russian airbase just inside the border, where the plane was stormed and the Ovechkins killed or captured.

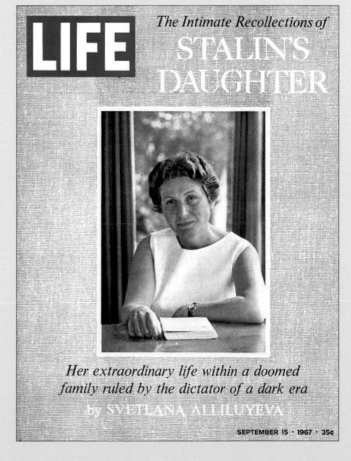

The Intimate Recollections of
STALIN'S DAUGHTER
Her extraordinary life within a doomed family ruled by the dictator of a dark era
by SVETLANA ALLILUYEVA
SEPTEMBER 15 · 1967 · 35¢

Right: Svetlana Alliluyeva's defection to the United States was a major coup.

9

'WE WILL BURY YOU'

Stalin's passing ushered in a comparatively calmer phase in Soviet history, although life in Russia had not changed in its essentials.

'We will bury you...!' Nikita Khrushchev (1894–1971) promised an audience of Western correspondents in Moscow in November 1956 – a particularly tetchy time in East–West relations. Was it a threat to immolate the NATO countries in a nuclear holocaust? Or simply a prediction: that the USSR would outlast its enemies and endure long after capitalism had (in Marxist terms) been brought down by its own 'contradictions'? To this day, that question is disputed, although it is of exclusively historical interest now, the Soviet Union having interred itself three decades since.

Khrushchev's irascibility (his other great claim to fame is having taken off his shoe to bang his desktop while attacking capitalism's lackeys at the General Assembly of the United Nations in New York in 1960) smacks of defensiveness, at least in hindsight. At the time, it carried an implicit suggestion of World War III, so few in the West felt confident enough to triumph.

Opposite: Moscow's May Day parades were watched closely by a suspicious – sometimes anxious – outside world. They were as much a show of strength as a celebration.

'HELP HUNGARY!'

Above: Soviet tanks patrol a junction in Budapest.

KHRUSHCHEV'S IRRITABILITY IN the autumn of 1956 is partly explained by his embarrassment over recent events within the Soviet bloc. That October, a student protest in Budapest had escalated into a nationwide uprising against a government that, although nominally Hungarian, only too obviously took its orders from the Kremlin. A heavy-handed reaction from state authorities, who shot at the demonstrators, sparked a deepening and broadening of the protest movement.

By Western standards, the revolt seemed to have a socialist, Soviet-style flavour: workers' councils were set up in workplaces and town halls. A new Free Hungary was proclaimed, although its leader, Imre Nagy (1896–1958), was a long-time communist, albeit of a fairly liberal, free-thinking kind.

At the beginning of November, the Soviet Union sent in tanks to restore order. Popular militias fought bravely for several days and more than 2500 freedom fighters were killed. The West was reluctant to get involved, despite appeals for help over national radio. Soon a new and loyal (to Russia) premier had been installed. Under János Kádár (1912–89), normal Soviet-style service was resumed in Hungary: some 7000 Party members were purged.

Hardliners in Moscow were not slow in blaming Khrushchev and his softening of political discipline: give the people an inch, and they'll take a mile, they reasoned. Certainly, when a similar situation boiled up in Czechoslovakia 12 years later, Leonid Brezhnev would not pussyfoot around.

Khrushchev's bark was worse than his bite. By recent Soviet standards, indeed, he was a radical reformer, bent on bringing Russia out of the darkness in which Stalin had entombed it. His programme of 'De-Stalinization' didn't just bring an end to the late leader's cult of personality – pulling down statues, removing his name from public buildings, monuments, and the national anthem; it set about dismantling his legacy in more substantial ways, starting with the gulags. They did not disappear completely, but the number was massively reduced and the conditions eased. The Soviet Union still would not be an open arena for the free expression of views, but neither would it run on paranoia.

STALIN HAD MADE TERROR AN INSTRUMENT OF GOVERNMENT. THAT COULDN'T BE SUSTAINED IN THE LONGER TERM.

PARTY MAN

Khrushchev may have been bad-tempered, but so benign was his reign by comparison with what had gone before that the temptation is to imagine him as kind and cuddly. He does deserve credit for his reforms, even if he introduced them for the sake of the USSR's survival.

Stalin had made terror an instrument of government. That couldn't be sustained in the long term. From the Kremlin corridors to the factory floor, the fear of being denounced, and the pressure to denounce others pre-emptively, had left Soviet society in a state of scarcely containable anxiety and stress.

In fairness, if far-reaching reform was Khrushchev's only practical choice, it was still the right one. But if Khrushchev's

Below: The notorious 'shoe-banging' incident at the United Nations in 1960 didn't do Khrushchev any favours: his performance smacked more of petulance than of power.

Above: He may have broken with his legacy, but Khrushchev had been a loyal henchman in Stalin's lifetime.

enlightenment merits recognition, so does his cognizance of – and complicity in – the evil done in Stalin's name.

As a Party boss in Moscow through the 1930s, Khrushchev had been a vociferous supporter of Stalin's purges. He had done his bit in condemning so-called *kulaks* living in the city (the idea of an urban peasant is oxymoronic enough to underline the absurdity of the Party's persecution) to arrest and execution. He had gone beyond the call of duty, having more than 40,000 suspects rounded up. More than 8000 of these were shot, more or less on Khrushchev's say-so.

ROCKET SCIENCE

It seems harsh to take the Soviets to task for developing nuclear weapons when they were following in the wake of their Western enemies in doing so. There is a certain darkness about the part played by espionage in that development: Russia relied on spies within the Manhattan Project – most famously Klaus Fuchs (1911–88) – and afterwards on agents such as the Rosenbergs

(Ethel, 1915–53, and Julius, 1918–53). However, not long afterwards, President John F. Kennedy (1917–63) was boasting openly of America's capacity to destroy the Soviet Union twice over.

As for the so-called 'Space Race', which dominated the news by the end of the 1950s, few really doubted that this was just the 'Arms Race' by other means. If the Soviet Union was hypocritical in suggesting that their Sputnik satellite and Soyuz space missions were really about the universal betterment of humankind, the Americans (after their initial shock at being beaten into orbit) were every bit as pious in their pronouncements.

Above: Klaus Fuchs served Stalin from within the Manhattan Project.

KHRUSHCHEV AND CUBA

One major incident of the Cold War was the Cuban Missile Crisis of 1962. Satellite evidence received on 16 October showed that Soviet ballistic missiles, capable of carrying nuclear warheads, were being moved into position on the Caribbean island for installation some 160km (100 miles) from the

METRO MAN

KHRUSHCHEV'S CAREER OFFERS **further reminders that, even in its real achievements, the Soviet system was soaked in blood. Built between 1932 and 1934, the Moscow Metro was billed as being the 'world's greatest' in both beauty and efficiency; in its final form, it didn't fall too far short. One of the truly impressive accomplishments of Soviet communism, it was completed in an astonishingly short time thanks to Khrushchev's energy and**

drive – and his readiness to sacrifice the safety of Soviet workers.

The statistics are still secret, but there were many accidents and injuries, and strong suspicions that hundreds of labourers were killed. As time went on, moreover, it began to emerge that corner cutting in construction had led to problems in the running of the system and to the undermining of foundations, sewers and water mains above.

Above: All-out nuclear war was unthinkable, so the Cold War superpowers found ways of attacking each other via 'proxy wars' like this one in Korea.

continental United States. No American administration could afford to appear weak in such a situation, but Kennedy's was already compromised after its mishandling of the 'invasion' at the Bay of Pigs. It stood accused not only of incompetence but of cowardice, having supposedly supported the émigrés involved before backing out without warning at the final moment. The exiles had made their landing only to find the promised US air cover absent and Cuba's armed forces very much present, in overwhelming force: more than 100 of the rebels had been killed.

America's irritation at this Soviet mischief-making in its Caribbean backyard was understandable, even if its indignation (given the installation of its own ballistic missiles in Italy and Turkey) perhaps wasn't. What really mattered, however, was the maintenance of immediate security, and of international 'face' in the longer term. As US naval ships moved to blockade Cuba, Kennedy and Khrushchev faced off in a high-strategy poker game, with the very real prospect of triggering nuclear war.

Hindsight may help us see more clearly, but it cannot enable us to fully appreciate the nerve-shredding tension of those days in 1962. Not till 27 October did Kennedy agree to remove his missiles from the USSR's borders secretly; Khrushchev gave the order for his to go the next day. The Russian premier had arguably got exactly what he wanted. However, his climbdown had been public and JFK's hadn't, so Khrushchev's position was

PLAYING DOMINOES

THE FIRST OF A series of proxy wars between the communist East and capitalist West had been fought in Korea, but there were many other conflicts in the Cold War era. The 'nuclear balance' may have saved the world from all-out war, but at the same time it guaranteed the channelling of US and Soviet resources and influence into more localized conflicts with less at stake in terms of life and death (for them at least).

Opinions differ on exactly when Fidel Castro (1926–2016) threw in his lot with Soviet communism. It was probably within a few months after the revolution in 1959 in which he and his supporters overthrew Cuba's dictator Fulgencio Batista (1901–73). The years that followed saw the superpowers sparring at arm's length in arenas from the Latin American mainland to southeast Asia, from the islands of Melanesia to southern Africa. Across the Third World, formerly colonialized countries had been breaking free, but had yet to finalize the ideological courses they would take.

US strategists argued that, should one state fall to communism, another in its vicinity was likely to follow its example, then another and another – and so on, like a row of collapsing dominoes. The domino theory was much ridiculed by liberal and left-wing thinkers – and it *was* ridiculous, if taken too literally, as some law of geopolitical mechanics.

However, there is no doubt that the success of one liberation struggle would likely inspire those struggling in other countries; nor were triumphant revolutionaries likely to begrudge like-minded comrades in neighbouring nations a helping hand. Pronounced in 1968, the Brezhnev Doctrine made the Soviet Union's support for such struggles a priority – and set the stage for further confrontations.

to be much weaker from that time on. Two years later, indeed, he was toppled to make way for Leonid Brezhnev (1906–82).

BACK TO THE FUTURE

As his comrades had intended, Brezhnev dialled down the thermostat on the so-called 'Khrushchev Thaw', bringing his predecessor's programme of liberalization to a close. Without returning to the insanity of the Stalin era, he made the Soviet Union uncomfortable for dissidents, as the novelist Alexander Solzhenitsyn (1918–2008) and the nuclear physicist-turned-peace-campaigner Andrei Sakharov (1921–89) were to find. Wayward nations fared just as badly: the Prague Spring quickly turned chilly when tanks were sent into a would-be reformist Czechoslovakia in 1968.

Brezhnev also returned the Soviet Union to its former hostile footing with regards to the West, making military strength and

Below: The 'invasion' of Cuba at the Bay of Pigs ended up in a complete fiasco. Here captive 'freedom fighters' are marched away by Castro's troops.

political security priorities. In the years that followed, the USSR matched America step for step in the nuclear arms race, though at a considerable – and ultimately prohibitive – cost.

RUSSIA'S 'VIETNAM'

If the United States had 'dominoes', the Soviet Union had its own, down in the Caucasus. Here, in the 1970s, as before in the 18th century, Islam and nationalism were making common cause. Much the same was happening in Soviet Central Asia. In Tajikistan, Turkmenistan and Uzbekistan, traditionally Muslim peoples were inspired by the fight of Afghanistan's *mujahideen* ('Holy Muslim Warriors').

The monarchy that had since World War I sought to impose a Western-style modernity on Afghanistan had made heavy weather of opposition from conservative religious leaders and tribal chiefs. But the avowedly atheistic military clique who in the 1970s had seized power with Soviet backing had been a living, breathing, governing reproach to Allah. Hence the ferocity of the resistance now put up by the *mujahideen* – and the consequent need of the puppet government to appeal to its Muscovite mentors for help.

In 1979, the Soviets invaded the country. It was to be, as the cliché had it, their 'Vietnam'. Armed by their own patriotism and religious zeal and by the discreet generosity of the United States, the *mujahideen* kept up a merciless assault. In 1989, after the loss of around 15,000 Soviet soldiers, the Russians were forced to withdraw in ignominy.

Like the Americans in Vietnam, they had committed a fair few atrocities on the road to defeat. Like the Americans in Vietnam, they had struggled to distinguish the guerrilla fighters they were

Above: Writer Alexander Solzhenitsyn shocked the world with books like *The Gulag Archipelago* (1973). He had witnessed these realities at first hand.

STORM DAMAGE

THE RUSSIANS HAD A word for it: *shturmovshchina*, or 'storming' – that heroic, headlong rush to complete a plan. The Soviet system was ideal for mobilizing labour and resources on an enormous scale when there was a specific task to be accomplished – like the lightning-fast construction of the Moscow Metro. That example also underlines the limitations of the approach, of course: corners were cut and standards skimped so the headline target could be hit. Even the biggest private companies in a capitalist economy couldn't hope to take on enterprises on that sort of epic scale. But such output as they could

Left: Leonid Brezhnev restored a sort of Stalinism-lite.

muster they could sustain. Their shareholders weren't in it for the sake of any specific project but for a consistent and ongoing return.

Something of the same logic may be seen to prevail in all of the Soviet Union's real achievements: its victory in World War II, for instance. It was an extraordinary achievement, but bought at a horrendous cost by a leadership prepared to throw enormous resources (in this case human lives) at the problem. Afterwards, through the Cold War years, the USSR kept pace with the United States in building its nuclear arsenal despite the crippling price its people paid. One-quarter of the country's economic output went into the military, it has been estimated, compared with one-sixteenth of the United States' through that same period.

Left: Mighty ICBMs steal the show at Moscow's annual May Day parade.

actually at war with from the rural civilian population they moved and hid among. Like the Americans in Vietnam, they had been known not to let that distinction worry them too much and commit generalized massacres that had bordered on genocidal. (At least two million civilians are believed to have been killed.) Like the Americans in Vietnam, they had lain waste to villages and land to make them unavailable to their enemy – even though that meant making them unavailable to those who lived and farmed there. In addition came the abduction and rape of Afghan women – not just for sadistic 'fun' but to create shock and to disrupt a conservative village culture. Ultimately, this was all to very little purpose, except the inflammation of feeling in nearby Islamic countries, including several of their own supposedly 'Soviet' republics.

Below: The Soviet Union had supposedly represented the final triumph of the 'little guy' in history: Afghanistan's *mujahideen* showed just how wrong that was.

'POOR QUALITY'

'Our rockets can find Halley's comet,' said the Russian leader Mikhail Gorbachev in 1988, 'but many household appliances are of poor quality.' He was articulating one of the most important challenges the Soviet Union faced. Soviet communism had pulled off some extraordinary feats of economic and technological development; it had saved Russia (and, arguably, Europe) from Nazi rule. But it had failed to give its people, first, anything remotely resembling 'freedom', and second, a domestic and national infrastructure that actually worked.

Its ability to start in sub-zero temperatures apart, the Soviet national car, the AvtoVAZ Lada, was a joke. Russian consumer goods, from shoes to washing machines, were shoddy, when they could be secured at all. The mass of the people lived in bleak apartment blocks and had a dreary diet. But if the worker's paradise was less than paradisal, all had work, and absolute poverty was unknown. This was true, up to a point, although the masses in their modest sufficiency would have envied the plight of all but the poorest in the developed West.

> MUCH OF THE COUNTRY'S WIDER INFRASTRUCTURE HAD BEEN ABOUT AS USEFUL AS A THREE-FINGERED GLOVE TO START WITH.

Below: Regarded in Russia (and beyond) with a certain amused affection, the Lada's performance was hopelessly inadequate by Western standards.

It wasn't just the household appliances that were substandard. Much of the country's wider infrastructure had been about as useful as a three-fingered glove to start with and had since fallen into decrepitude like some broken fridge. In April 1986, for example, a reactor fire at the Chernobyl Nuclear Plant, north of Kiev, in Ukraine, had caused a large-scale leak of radiation. A mass evacuation had left nearby Pripyat a ghost town. A 10-km (6-mile) evacuation zone established in the

hours after the reactor fire had to be extended a few days later. Soon, more than 130,000 people had been removed from an area of around 30km (20 miles) around the plant.

This was the Soviet Union, and heroic helicopter pilots were available to fly into the heart of the radiation hazard and drop fire-retarding sand, clay and boron into the flames to quench the leak, after which construction workers toiled for days encasing the toxic mess within a concrete shell. It seems churlish to quibble at their courage and their social commitment – although it was quite in keeping with the spirit of Soviet history that the authorities should have thrown human lives at the problem in this way.

It is hard to know how many casualties the disaster caused. Although only a few hundred died in the first months and years after the leak, several million have complained of health problems in the years since. In the days following the fire, the radiation cloud was carried by the wind across Belorussia and on to northwest Europe – who knows what the long-term

Above: The rescue effort at Chernobyl showed Soviet values at their very best; but the disaster that prompted all this heroism highlighted the Revolution's failure.

10

OPENING UP AND CLOSING DOWN

A nightmarish episode ended with the fall of the Soviet Union –
but for Russian history, the darkness wasn't over.

THE BRITISH journalist Oliver Bullough was brutal in saying that the Soviet system was 'almost perfectly designed to make people unhappy', but it would be hard to claim convincingly that he was wrong. Leonid Brezhnev died in 1982, making way for a new premier, Yuri Andropov (1914–84) – till then chairman of the Commission for State Security or KGB. Another secret policeman at the head of the world's most powerful police state, he had been ambassador to Hungary in 1956. There was no sign of the Party loosening its hold.

There were unprecedented pressures, however. Even as the costs of the Afghan war were escalating, the United States was opening up a new and fantastically expensive front in the Cold War conflict with its Strategic Defense Initiative (SDI), or 'Star Wars'. The development of a protective shield against Intercontinental Ballistic Missiles (ICBMs) coordinated from satellites circling the Earth in orbit would shift the balance of military advantage dramatically. This shift would be irrevocable

Opposite: The Red Flag flew outside the White House for Mikhail Gorbachev's 1987 visit. Inside it was all smiles as the Soviet Premier and President Reagan posed for pictures.

Above: Yuri Andropov's career in the KGB had proved him to be both capable and ruthless – but neither quality could save the Soviet Union now.

unless the USSR developed its own equivalent system in time to cancel out the one that US President Ronald Reagan (1911–2004) had undertaken to establish.

OLD AND SICK

Andropov did his best to tackle his country's problems with a wholesale war on corruption. Necessary as this was, it didn't do enough. In 1983, he cancelled the USSR's own research into space-based weapons, and it was hard to present this as anything other than a Cold War climbdown. Relations with the West did not improve, however, and negotiations over arms limitation broke down – a further blow to a Soviet economy that badly needed to cut costs.

That a certain panic-stricken paralysis reigned at the top in Soviet governing circles can be inferred from the decision to have Andropov succeeded, on his death in 1984, by another elderly veteran, Konstantin Chernenko (1911–85). Chernenko was so sick himself that he could hardly speak to give the eulogy at Andropov's funeral. His reign as premier seems to have gone by in a fuddled haze.

REFORMIST REVOLUTION

Chernenko died in March 1985. This time, his successor was much younger: Mikhail Gorbachev (1931–). He had been a lifelong communist, but he came to office promising a policy of *Perestroika* – a wholesale restructuring of the political and economic system in the USSR. To allow that institutional transformation, an important shift in cultural sensibility was needed.

Gorbachev called this *glasnost*, or 'openness'. It amounted to greater freedom, of speech, publications and political activism, but also of entrepreneurship and business; for the first time since Lenin's NEP, private enterprise would be allowed. There were changes in diplomacy, too: Gorbachev made high-profile visits to the West. These were drastic changes, Gorbachev acknowledged, but they were necessary if a crisis-ridden Soviet Union was to be saved.

LICENSED TO KILL

ON 1 SEPTEMBER 1983, Korean Air Lines Flight 007 set off from New York bound for Seoul. Several hours later, it left Anchorage, Alaska, after a routine stop. For reasons that aren't generally known – and that have been debated ever since – it strayed off its regular flight path across the North Pacific. This was only a slight divergence, but it took the Boeing 747 well to the west of where it should have been. More specifically – and sinisterly – it took it over the south of the Soviet Union's sensitive Kamchatka Peninsula before it crossed the southern tip of the strategically important, and contentious, Sakhalin Island.

At this point, the pilot of one of four MiG-23 fighters, which had for some time been shadowing KAL007, shot the civilian airliner down as a supposed spy plane. He could see it was a 747, he acknowledged, but neither he nor his air traffic controllers had any reason to doubt its dodgy status given its lengthy flight in strictly prohibited airspace.

The downed airliner hit the ocean with the loss of 269 lives: for over 12 hours after its disappearance, while desperate families waited in Seoul for news, the Soviets denied any involvement in the plane's loss, and confusion reigned. To this day, conspiracy theorists insist that KAL007 must indeed have been on a spying mission, although a faulty autopilot remains the simplest explanation for its wanderings.

Right: Protesters in Seoul burn a Soviet flag after the downing of flight KAL007.

Above: Poland's 'Solidarity' movement was a sign of changing times across the Soviet sphere: workers wanted a freedom they couldn't see themselves finding under Communism.

It is hardly surprising that more conservative elements in the Communist Party felt Gorbachev was seeking to 'save' the system by abolishing it completely. By 1989, there were already signs of that system starting to crumble. In Poland, the free trade union 'Solidarity' had been a thorn in the communist government's flesh since 1980, an embarrassment to what claimed to be a workers' state. Now it defied the authorities by standing – and winning – in elections.

Hungary, meanwhile, was in a restive and rebellious mood. Demonstrations followed in Bulgaria and Czechoslovakia – the 'domino effect' in action. As East Germans took advantage of chaos in Hungary to escape across that country's borders to the West, the authorities in East Berlin began to lose control. By November 1989, crowds were swarming across no man's land, unhindered by guards, and, quite literally, pulling down the Berlin Wall.

FROM COUP TO COLLAPSE
In August 1991, communist hardliners tried to bring down Mikhail Gorbachev in a coup. Tanks surrounded the Russian

parliament building, the White House, but the citizens of Moscow turned out in force to protect the seat of such democracy as existed in their country. Gorbachev saw off the threat, with their support, though he still stood weakened.

The Soviet Union was weakened too: the weeks that followed saw several of its constituent republics breaking loose: Armenia, Belarus, Georgia, Kazakhstan, Kyrgyzstan, Moldova, Tajikistan, Turkmenistan, Ukraine and Uzbekistan. While nominally they remained within a Commonwealth of Independent States (CIS), the emphasis quickly came to be less on the idea of commonalty and more on that of independence. Russia itself became a federation of semi-autonomous subdivisions – cities and regional republics. Unthinkable as it was to a generation in the West (and, still more so to its own citizens) the Union of Soviet Socialist Republics was no more.

The presidency passed to Boris Yeltsin (1931–2007), a sometime Gorbachev protégé who had become a critic – not from the conservative, communist, side, but from a more radical free-market perspective. He delivered much of the reform he had promised, but the concentration of resources into a fairly small number of local and sectoral monopolies as big state enterprises were privatized was ripe for exploitation by a handful of foreign corporations or homegrown capitalists – often drawn from the ranks of former Soviet officials. Soon these buccaneering figures had grown so much in wealth and power that they were known as 'oligarchs'.

TOXIC TRANSITION
Although their wealth rocketed, that of the overall economy was hit by falling global prices for the kind of commodities

Below: Boris Yeltsin, George H. Bush and US First Lady Barbara Bush pose outside the White House during Yeltsin's state visit of 1992.

Russia produced (grain, timber, minerals), while many citizens were reduced to severe hardship. Corruption was rife, and spectacularly lucrative. Meanwhile, the dispossessed – their national resources sold out from under them – had constantly before their eyes the sight of their less scrupulous fellow citizens cruising the streets in fancy cars, falling out of nightclubs in designer suits, buying top-end furs and jewellery for their mistresses, even arranging to have their bodies embalmed, Lenin-style, after they died.

CRIME GETS ORGANIZED

ALONG WITH POLITICAL gangsterism, the more literal, nakedly criminal kind thrived in the political and social vacuum that followed the collapse of communism.

Freedom from crime had been one of the vaunted advantages of life in the Soviet Union. Like most of the supposed benefits of socialism, this freedom had been much exaggerated. Pilfering had been an everyday problem in everything from the military to industry, while the restrictiveness of the economy, and the scarcities this had brought, had created the conditions for a big black market in luxuries. It was true that the sort of street crime and open violence found in Western cities had largely been absent, but human nature was just the same here, despite the best efforts of the Party propagandists. More important, the structures – concentrated criminal gangs and wider networks of contacts through the economy – were already in place, firmly established and ready to exploit the chaos when it came.

The Russian Mafia that emerged in the 1990s was a loose assortment of small-scale gangs, cooperating with each other on an ad hoc basis and held together as much by opportunism as by ethnic or kinship ties. But that didn't make it any less dangerous or threatening in the aggregate, either at home in Russia or, increasingly, in Western Europe or the United States. By 1996, the Ministry of the Interior estimated, there were more than 8000 gangs, with 120,000 active members, in Russia alone, and more in over 40 countries overseas.

The mobs dealt in all the usual modern crime; the most sinister thing about the Russian gangsters, though, was the way in which, having been in at the beginnings of their country's capitalist economy, they had insinuated themselves into the very fabric of its 'legitimate' businesses and industries. More than 50,000 companies were believed to be controlled by gangs by 1996, accounting for 40 per cent of Russia's Gross National Product (GNP).

In hindsight, it is hard to see how a crisis of this kind could have been avoided. Russia had been under rigid socialist rule for 70 years. Now, all of a sudden, it was being expected to work as a fully functioning free-market economy. Quite simply, the body politic was not prepared.

CHANGE AT THE TOP

The situation only worsened as the months went by. Output plunged and prices surged. Inflation gave way to hyperinflation. Parliament opposed the privatization Yeltsin believed was needed. He dissolved the assembly, sparking widespread street protests, and what amounted to a sit-in by assembly members, who holed up in the White House and refused to be 'dissolved'. Yeltsin brought up tanks and soldiers and their protest was put down – although he had set an unfortunate precedent for a leader who claimed to be re-establishing democratic rule. By 1999, Yeltsin was forced to resign as president in favour of his prime minister, Vladimir Putin (1952–). Putin was known only as a Yeltsin loyalist. Time would show that he was very much his own man.

Above: Yeltsin's troops take back the Russian Parliament Building – occupied by its own assembly-members during the constitutional crisis of 1993.

11

THE BEAR IS BACK

Recent years have seen Russia's re-emergence as a force in world affairs – and, say many Western commentators, as a threat.

A SINKING ship is too obvious a metaphor to be missed. When it happens during a would-be re-emergent superpower's first large-scale naval exercise in over a decade, that only makes things worse. When its sister vessels register the initial explosion but don't even think to investigate, it starts to look like systemic carelessness. When, the situation at last acknowledged, it takes rescuers four days to gain access to the wreck, after successive much-hyped but ultimately abortive efforts, it casts the country responsible in a hopeless light.

When, in August 2000, the submarine *Kursk* went down with all 118 crew members in Arctic waters a few miles off Murmansk, the disaster seemed symbolic of Russia's post-Soviet decline. The victory at Kursk had been a bright spot in the country's history, but the name would have darker associations from now on.

Vladimir Putin had been elected as someone who could take charge of the country, act with toughness and decisiveness and

Opposite: Under the sponsorship of outgoing President Yeltsin, Vladimir Putin takes the presidential oath beneath the crest of the Russian Federation.

get things done. This was not the best advertisement for his regime. In another country, the president's background as an officer of the Soviet KGB might have put his public off, but, exhausted by their years of just about continuous crisis and confusion, Russians had been longing for firm government.

A CHALLENGE FROM CHECHNYA

Fortunately for him (if not necessarily for his country), Putin was to have his chance before too long. The challenge, and the opportunity, came from the Caucasus. As we've seen, the Chechens had – in common with other traditionally Muslim nations in Russia and beyond – been growing increasingly restless over recent years. They had never really accepted Russian rule, and had indeed fought bitterly for their freedom as far back as the 18th century.

They had been fighting again, hoping to take advantage of an apparent power vacuum in Moscow, since 1999; Russia's brutal reaction had only alienated Chechens further. More than 360 civilians had been killed in an air and artillery attack on one village alone: Katyr-Yurt, west of the Chechen capital Grozny. Rape and murder were routine in a campaign clearly intended to create an atmosphere of terror across the countryside.

Below: Having broken the hold of rebels over Gudermes, Chechnya's second city, Russian troops waste no time in setting about mopping up resistance.

THEATRE OF WAR

Unable to match the Russians in strength, Chechen fighters turned to terrorist attacks. On 23 October 2002, a band of armed men stormed Moscow's Dubrovka Theatre, mid-performance, taking cast and audience hostage – 850 men, women and children. When, after a four-day standoff, the attackers started killing

captives, special forces rushed the theatre. It was not the ideal arena for close-quarters fighting. Although all 40 terrorists were killed, so were 133 hostages.

In 2004, in Beslan, North Ossetia (a small, semi-autonomous region in the Russian Caucasus), Chechen rebels were joined by separatists from Ingushetia – another want-away Muslim region. Altogether, 34 attackers seized control of School Number One in the town, taking staff and students hostage – over a thousand people. Again, special forces stormed the site; again, they killed most of the terrorists; again, a great many hostages (380-odd) were killed.

These arguably excessive responses sent a clear message to Russia's internal enemies – and, maybe more importantly, to Russia's voters. Putin put himself forward as a protector and as a tough, no-nonsense strongman. Russians were regaled with press photos showing a bare-torsoed premier riding a horse, hunting, fishing, swimming in a rushing river…performing a whole range of stereotypically manly tasks in wild settings. While causing amusement in the West, these don't seem to have alienated their intended Russian audience. Putin's position only grew in strength

Above: October 2017, and 15 years after the attack on Moscow's Dubrovka Theatre, relatives still gather to commemorate those who died.

GAY RIGHTS AND WRONGS

CYNICAL OBSERVERS IN THE West (and, if maybe more discreetly, in Russia too) have not been slow to snigger at the 'homoerotic' overtones of Putin's shirtless portraits. The irony is particularly enjoyed because the Russian president's insistent manliness has gone along with an official intolerance towards LGBT+ rights.

In this, it must be acknowledged, Putin's views have been shared with the mass of people in a country long conservative on such issues. Laws introduced in 2013 to prohibit 'homosexual propaganda', nominally for the protection of minors, effectively threatened to outlaw serious writing on issues of sexuality, and, if officials chose, any significant organization and campaigning for the rights of sexual minority groups in Russia.

Left: The Pin-Up President: Vladimir Putin exudes manliness in another shirtless outdoor action shot.

THE UNACCEPTABLE FACE?

Ukraine had its 'Orange Revolution' at the end of 2004 and the first few weeks of 2005. The protests followed national elections that were widely believed to have been rigged by officials in favour of the Russian-supporting winner, Viktor Yanukovych (1950–). As government candidate, he was standing against the independent Viktor Yushchenko (1954–), a liberal who enjoyed the backing of the West. His aim, for Ukraine to join Western economic and strategic alliances, including NATO, put him at odds with the Putin regime.

Amid cries of foul and clamour for a re-run, that avenue was abruptly cut off by Yushchenko's collapse with a grave but mysterious illness. Hideous lesions appeared across his face, and he faded quickly and almost fatally with acute pancreatitis before doctors diagnosed dioxin poisoning. Toxicologists found 1000 times the permitted amount in his bloodstream. Yushchenko was fortunate to survive. Although the origin of the poison is obscure, he himself was in no doubt that it had been administered by agents of a Russian government eager to prevent any closer rapprochement between Ukraine and Western Europe.

SHOWING WHO'S BOSS

Putin's belligerent way with former Soviet republics was replicated in his relationship with the country's oligarchs. Within Russia, he had pretty much made himself dictator. Crucial had been his decision in 2000 – with the implicit acceptance of his electorate – to award himself the right to hire and fire previously elected regional governors. The step was essential, he argued, given the extent of corruption and even gangsterism in regional politics and the growing influence of secessionist movements in some areas. These were fair points, although this solution concentrated an enormous amount of power in Putin. It could only be hoped that his despotism would prove benevolent in the longer run.

Few felt there was anything disturbing about Putin's attacks on the country's oligarchs. There was widespread resentment of their wealth and power. Curbing those became not just a duty but a pleasure for Putin in the case of Mikhail Khodorkovsky (1963–), an oil magnate who had campaigned for freedom of expression, against the control of the media and other institutions by the executive, and against the corruption that kept the wheels of economic life going round in Putin's Russia.

Below: To this day, Ukrainian statesman Viktor Yushchenko bears the scars of having tried to face down Russian power in his country's 'Orange Revolution'.

In 2003, Khodorkovsky was accused of being corrupt himself, arrested and detained on what supporters insisted were trumped-up charges. Found guilty by a compliant court, he became one of Russian history's more improbable political prisoners. He was released in 2013, and went into exile.

SENSITIVE TO CRITICISM

Not surprisingly, perhaps, Putin has shown a secret policeman's attitude to media coverage, liking it upbeat, uncritical and essentially incurious about what is going on. It has been suggested that the murder in Moscow, on 7 October 2006, of Anna Politkovskaya (1958–2006), who was shot in the lift of her apartment building, was arranged on his orders. Having survived a poisoning attempt in 2004, Politkovskaya had persevered in reporting Russian atrocities in Chechnya – not the kind of

WHEELS WITHIN WHEELS, WARS WITHIN WARS

HAVING ITSELF BROKEN FREE of Russian domination in its Rose Revolution of 2003, Georgia faced the secession of South Ossetia – a tiny territory on its border with the Russian Federation. Ossetian nationalists had tried to set this state up in 1991, after the collapse of the Soviet Union, going to war with a newly independent Georgia.

By 2008, seeing South Ossetia's continuing claims as destabilizing Georgia, the Russians were happy to lend their support. South Ossetians carried out a campaign of ethnic cleansing, driving out Georgian families in their tens of thousands. Today, South Ossetia remains 'free' – though as far as Tbilisi is concerned, it is still very much a part of Georgia. It is a client state, carried economically by Russia.

Right: Job done. Russian tanks withdraw from South Ossetia, 2008.

coverage Putin's government appreciated.

The president had also ordered a hit on Boris Berezovsky (1946–2013), it was alleged. The media tycoon's newspapers and TV stations had kept up a fairly constant stream of criticism of Putin's government and eventually he had taken himself into an English exile. In 2013, he was found hanged at his new home in Sunningdale, Berkshire – seemingly by suicide, although the British coroner still returned an open verdict.

Putin's accuser in the cases both of Politkovskaya and Berezovsky had been the former KGB/Federal Security Bureau (FSB) officer Alexander Litvinenko (1962–2006). He himself had defected to England after making these claims and, granted asylum there, seemed set for further damaging revelations about the Russian leadership. Then, in November 2006, he suddenly fell ill and died a few weeks later. He was found to have been poisoned with radioactive Polonium 210. British investigators identified Andrey Lugovoy (1966–) as their main suspect – he had met with Litvinenko on the day he'd fallen ill – but the authorities in Moscow refused to extradite him.

Above: Enemy of the People? Or just of Putin? Mikhail Khodorkovsky stands, unsurprised, as his sentence is read out in Moscow's Meschansky District Court.

THE BEAR REAWAKENS

Concern was growing in the wider world that, its recent decades of turmoil having left Russia out of things, the bear was reawakening from its hibernation. The conflict with Ukraine was deepening. Russia had not been impressed by the Revolution of February 2014 in which Yushchenko's nemesis, Viktor Yanukovych, had at last been ousted. Putin took advantage of the confusion to send in troops to annex Crimea, over which Russia had for a long time maintained a claim. Relations continued to be tetchy: Russia cut off Ukraine's gas supplies after a dispute in 2014, at much the same time as fighting was getting under way between Russian-backed anti-government militias and Ukrainian forces in the Donetsk and Luhansk districts.

For the most part a forgotten (if not an unnoticed) war in the West, this conflict hit the headlines internationally when, on 17 July that year, militiamen shot down a Malaysian Airlines' Boeing 777 en route from Amsterdam to Kuala Lumpur with the loss of all 298 people on board.

A disturbing situation in itself, the crisis in Syria from 2011 onwards was seen by some as showing Putin's Russia reaching beyond the borders of the former USSR to impose its will. This was only to be expected: Syria had been Russia's staunchest Middle Eastern ally

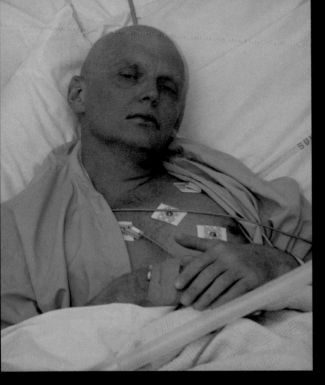

Above: Alexander Litvinenko dies in a London hospital, 2006. He had accused his former FSB superiors in the killing of Boris Berezovsky.

since Soviet times, when it was ruled by President Hafez Al-Assad (1930–2000), a sworn enemy of the United States and its Israeli 'policeman' in the region. Under his son Bashar Al-Assad (1965–) and his Ba'athist government, the country remained a redoubt of old-fashioned Arab Nationalism (left-wing and essentially secularist) in what was by now a rapidly Islamicizing region. Radical Islamism had been rocking the Russian boat for decades now, not just in Afghanistan but in the Caucasus as well.

When Bashar Al-Assad came under attack from domestic Jihadists, the West to some extent shared Putin's sympathy with him. Their feelings changed, though, with the revelation of large-scale atrocities and human rights violations by Assad (and of the closeness of his relationship with Russia). Putin's claim that Assad represented the lesser of two evils is by no means absurd, but critical commentators remained uneasy. The sense that, after a couple of decades on the back foot, a resurgent Russia was pursuing an expansionist path sowed consternation in governments and media in the West.

MISCHIEF MAKING

History repeats itself, communism's founder Karl Marx notoriously observed: the first time as tragedy, the second time as farce. It is not clear which of those categories Cold War II falls into. Or Cold War 2.0, for in this renewed opposition between Russian East and US-led West, one of the main weapons systems has been the personal computer and a major arena of conflict cyberspace.

PUTIN'S CLAIM THAT ASSAD REPRESENTED THE LESSER OF TWO EVILS IS BY NO MEANS ABSURD.

People mocked the paranoia of the Cold War era, when the Russians arrested and interrogated snapshot-taking tourists, while citizens in small-town America would sense the hand of Moscow in the breaking of a garden gnome. But, with Russian hackers seemingly spying on and sabotaging Western business systems, and 'bots' (or robots) planting pretend-vox-pop pronouncements on Twitter and 'fake news' items on Facebook and other social media, it has begun to appear that no area of everyday life is too trivial or obscure to be singled out for interference.

Not that the ultimate aims are trivial: while they themselves have strenuously denied it, US intelligence sources have asserted with 'high confidence' that agencies related to the Russian government waged a covert campaign to undermine the Democratic candidate Hillary Clinton (1947–) in the 2016 US presidential election. 'Fake news' stories of the tidal waves of job-taking, terrorist-sympathizing, crime-committing, Christmas-abolishing refugees she had let into the country were scattered across social media, while her campaign leaders' emails were mysteriously sent to the international online whistleblowing website WikiLeaks. How far the beneficiary of this interference, Donald Trump (1946–), and his supporters might have colluded with and assisted such measures was still being explored by a Special Counsel Investigation two years later.

It has also been alleged that Russian hackers have weighed in to weaken Western Europe by destabilizing its democracies, discreetly backing far-right and ultra-Nationalistic groups fomenting anti-immigrant unrest. It is both the beauty and the bane of the internet that it allows almost complete anonymity to its user (or in the case of the automated message-generating 'bot', the user's user), so such allegations are all but impossible to prove.

RUSSIA TODAY; TOMORROW THE WORLD?

ESTABLISHED IN 2005, WITH a big, young, lively (and well-funded) staff, the *Russia Today* TV station offered entertaining coverage of international affairs. No secret was made of its funding by the Russian government. Even so, its energetic and colourful presentation of world news from a different and openly non-Western perspective appealed to viewers around the world who felt their official broadcasters represented only establishment interests in their countries.

Above: Russia Today covers Vladimir Putin's meeting with President Donald Trump – Russia's 'useful idiot', some have charged.

The channel had been quick to spot the potential openings to a younger Western audience used to customizing their own consumption of media of every kind. Where their parents had simply switched on the TV or radio to hear an authoritative-sounding speaker tell them 'Here is the news …', these viewers saw the media as a supermarket from which they could pick and choose.

They were well aware that *Russia Today* was government-funded, but believed the same might be said of Britain's BBC, while other media represented only the millionaires who owned them. While conservative and centrist commentators might condemn those more outlying leaders of the left and right who appeared on (or even hosted) *Russia Today* shows, their followers appreciated the alternative perspectives the channel afforded them.

BEAR OR BASKET CASE?

The best-informed Western commentators cannot agree on the exact nature and ultimate aims of the Putin project. Some suggest that the Russian president is rebuilding Imperial Russia as an authoritarian quasi-USSR that won't rest until it has made itself the dominant force in Europe and beyond. For others, this warmongering, world-threatening Putin is a pantomime villain, conjured up by the Western elite.

There are other takes too. We are right to fear Vladimir Putin, argues the British-French journalist Ben Judah. He is a 'strongman' precisely because he is weak. At least one Russian writer agrees with Judah: 'If you compare the post-Soviet bear to the Soviet one,' says novelist Vladimir Sorokin (1955–), 'the only thing they have in common is the imperial roar.' What we see as strength is really no more than empty bellicosity, Sorokin suggests; what seems a flexing of muscles is merely so much neurotic twitching.

Above: In March 2018, the former spy Sergei Skripal and his daughter were struck down by a nerve agent in Salisbury, England: Prime Minister Theresa May blamed Putin's Russia.

The post-Soviet bear is teeming with corrupt parasites that infected it during the 1990s, and have multiplied exponentially in the last decade. They are consuming the bear from within. Some might mistake their fevered movement under the bear's hide for the working of powerful muscles. But in truth, it's an illusion. There are no muscles, the bear's teeth have worn down, and its brain is buffeted by the random firing of contradictory neurological impulses: 'Get rich!' 'Modernize!' 'Steal!' 'Pray!' 'Build Great Mother Russia!' 'Resurrect the USSR!' 'Beware of the West!' 'Invest in Western real estate!' 'Keep your savings in dollars and euros!' 'Vacation in Courchevel!' 'Be patriotic!' 'Search and destroy the enemies within!'

Time will tell whether the West has anything to fear from Russia. It seems safe to assume, though, that for the Russians, one way or another, the darkness is destined to go on.

BIBLIOGRAPHY

Applebaum, Anne, *Gulag: A History of the Soviet Camps* (London: Allen Lane, 2003).

— *Gulag Voices: An Anthology* (New Haven, CT: Yale, 2011).

— *Iron Curtain: The Crushing of Eastern Europe, 1944–56* (London: Penguin, 2012).

Beevor, Antony, *Berlin: The Downfall, 1945* (London: Viking, 2002).

Bennett, Vanora, *Crying Wolf: The Return of War to Chechnya* (Second revised edition, London: Pan, 2011).

Bullough, Oliver, *The Last Man in Russia: And the Struggle to Save a Dying Nation* (London: Allen Lane, 2013).

Bushkovitch, Paul, *A Concise History of Russia* (Cambridge: CUP, 2012).

Dukes, Paul, *The Making of Russian Absolutism, 1613–1801* (London: Routledge, 1990).

Dwork, Debórah, and Van Pelt, Robert Jan, *Holocaust: A History* (London: John Murray, 2002).

Haslam, Jonathan, *Russia's Cold War* (New Haven, CT: Yale, 2011).

Longworth, Philip, *Russia's Empires: Their Rise and Fall from Prehistory to Putin* (London: John Murray, 2005).

Madariaga, Isabel de, *Ivan the Terrible* (New Haven, CT: Yale, 2005).

Merridale, Catherine, *Ivan's War: Inside the Red Army, 1939–45* (London, 2005).

Overy, Richard, *Russia's War: Blood Upon the Snow* (London: Penguin, 1997).

Pipes, Richard, *Russia Under the Old Regime* (London: Penguin, 1995).

Reid, Anna, *Borderland: A Journey Through the History of Ukraine* (London: Orion, 1999).

— *The Shaman's Coat: The People of Siberia* (London: Weidenfeld & Nicolson, 2002).

— *Leningrad: Tragedy of a City Under Siege, 1941–44* (London: Bloomsbury, 2011).

Roosevelt, Priscilla, *Life on the Russian Country Estate: A Social and Cultural History* (New Haven, CT: Yale, 1995).

Satter, David, *It was a Long Time Ago, and it Never Happened Anyway: Russia and the Communist Past* (New Haven, CT: Yale, 2012).

Sebag-Montefiore, Simon, *The Romanovs* (London: Weidenfeld & Nicolson, 2015).

— *Prince of Princes: The Life of Potemkin* (London: Weidenfeld & Nicolson, 2000).

— *Young Stalin* (London: Weidenfeld & Nicolson, 2007).

— *Stalin: The Court of the Red Tsar* (London: Weidenfeld & Nicolson, 2003).

Service, Robert, *The Penguin History of Modern Russia: From Tsarism to the Twenty-First Century* (London: Penguin, 2015).

— *Lenin: A Biography* (London: Macmillan, 2000).

— *Stalin: A Biography* (London: Macmillan, 2005).

— *Trotsky: A Biography* (London: Macmillan, 2010).

Smith, S.A., *Russia in Revolution: An Empire in Crisis, 1890–1928* (Oxford: OUP, 2017).

Steinberg, Mark D., and Khrustalëv, Vladimir M., *The Fall of the Romanovs: Political Dreams and Personal Struggles in a Time of Revolution* (New Haven, CT: Yale, 1997).

Thubron, Colin, *In Siberia* (London: Vintage, 2007).

Ure, John, *The Cossacks* (London: Constable, 1999).

Volkov, Solomon, tr. Bouis, Antonia W., *Shostakovich and Stalin* (London: Little, Brown, 2004).

Waldron, Peter, *Russia of the Tsars* (London: Thames & Hudson, 2011).

Wasserstein, Bernard, *On the Eve: The Jews of Europe Before the Second World War* (London: Profile, 2012).

Zamoyski, Adam, *1812: Napoleon's Fatal March on Moscow* (London: HarperCollins, 2004).

INDEX

PICTURE CREDITS